This book is for dads who understand that their chil[...] be both cherished and nourished.

Peter Nanfelt
president, Christian & Missionary Alliance

As you search for knowledge and inspiration on how to become a godly parent-educator and trainer of your children you can do no better than study the Bible-centered principles of this book.

Paul A. Kienel
founder and president emeritus, Association of Christians Schools International

This is not merely a "how to" manual on parenting. It is much more in that the important concepts presented are drawn from Scripture and illustrated in a practical format with powerful personal illustrations.

Dennis E. Williams
dean of institutional assessment, Southern Baptist Seminary

This is a thoughtful book that stimulates productive thinking, provides helpful insights, and interests readers about biblical fathering. Outstanding, instructive, creative, and biblically sound. Recommended for fathers, families, youth groups, and study groups.

Byrle Kynerd
headmaster, Briarwood Christian School

Could a book such as this be more appropriate for the community of believers? Our culture needs the message of this book. Kenn and Jeff Gangel have touched a vital nerve for every father or would-be-father. Warm illustrations and honest reflections frame the powerful and timely message of this book for every Christian father. The plausibility of the message is validated by the credibility of the life experiences of this father and son team.

Steven C. Babbit
director of publishing services, Association of Christian Schools International

The Gangels are a father and son team who've done all us dads a great service. They've brought us sound biblical teaching, powerful principles, and practical suggestions on how to build healthy lifelong relationships with our children. *Fathering Like the Father* provides the essential ingredients to help us be the kind of fathers that all of us yearn to be. As the father of four teenagers and a younger adopted orphan I know it will be a constant companion to me, providing wisdom and guidance from two men that have navigated these choppy waters before me. Thanks for leading the way!

Steve Shadrach
South Central director, Student Mobilization

Here's a uniquely helpful guide for the task and privilege of fathering. It's unique because a father and son have teamed up to share their insights. It's unique because, while psychologically well-informed, it deals biblically with a dad's responsibilities and opportunities applying to our very human problem the wisdom of our Father-God.

Vernon Grounds
chancellor, Denver Seminary

Solidly biblical, practical, timely, and refreshing. *Refreshing* because it's not a "Shame on you dads, you're not measuring up to God's standard for being a dad." Instead, the reader is drawn into the life events of a father and son and resonates with the interaction and relational commitment found in each other as best friends. As I read the material, I found myself cheering them on and saying, "Here are two men I would love to hang around with—this is as it should be between a father and son."

James L. Clark
director of the Biblical Counseling and Education Center, Calvary Bible College and Theological Seminary

Drs. Kenneth and Jeffrey Gangel have given us a fine volume on how fathers and sons can nurture a close and satisfying relationship with each other based on a scriptural foundation. This father and son duo give practical illustrations from their own lives as well as from broad reading in this area. This book encourages the strong bonds that will give a lifetime of rewards. Drink deeply at this forty-year flowing fount!

Warren S. Benson
former vice president of doctoral programs, Trinity Evangelical Divinity School

In his prayer for the Ephesian believers (Eph. 3:14ff), the apostle Paul intimates that the human notion of fatherhood has as its antecedent our matchless Heavenly Father. The question, "What would my Heavenly Father do?" has been a powerful force in guiding and shaping my own relationship to my two children for over 20 years now. I am so pleased that Kenn and Jeff Gangel have produced this biblically sound and culturally relevant study of our Heavenly Father's parenting patterns. My limited observation of Kenn's relationship with Jeff and Jeff's relationship with his young children convinces me that their message is accompanied by the authentic marks of *Fathering Like the Father*.

Ralph Enlow
provost, Columbia International University

Kenn and Jeff Gangel have collaborated on a marvelous work that takes a unique look at fathering and does it in a biblically correct and personally profitable way. Dr. Gangel has ministered to the church over the years with numerous books on Christian education and leadership, but this one is perhaps his finest contribution. From a wealth of biblical knowledge and demonstrated effective living, Kenn and Jeff share their passion, their perspective, and practical guidance for effective godly living for Christian fathers everywhere.

Gilbert A. Peterson
chancellor, Lancaster Bible College

FATHERING
LIKE THE FATHER

Other books by Kenneth O. Gangel

Feeding and Leading

Volunteers for Today's Church (coauthored with Dennis Williams)

Your Family (coauthored with Betty Gangel)

Team Leadership in Christian Ministry

Ministering to Today's Adults

Coaching Ministry Teams

The Christian Educator's Handbook on Teaching (coedited with Howard G. Hendricks)

The Christian Educator's Handbook on Adult Education (coedited with James Wilhoit)

The Christian Educator's Handbook on Family Life Education (coedited with James Wilhoit)

FATHERING
LIKE THE FATHER

Becoming the Dad
God Wants You to Be

Kenneth O. Gangel
and Jeffrey S. Gangel

 Baker Books

A Division of Baker Book House Co
Grand Rapids, Michigan 49516

Published by Baker Books
a division of Baker Book House Company
P.O. Box 6287, Grand Rapids, MI 49516-6287
www.bakerbooks.com

Second printing, May 2003

Printed in the United States of America

Library of Congress Cataloging-in-Publication Data

Gangel, Kenneth O.
    Fathering like the Father : becoming the dad God wants you to be / Kenneth Gangel and Jeffrey Gangel.
        p.   cm.
    Includes bibliographical references.
    ISBN 0-8010-6432-5 (pbk.)
        1. Fatherhood—Religious aspects—Christianity. 2 Fatherhood—Biblical teaching. 3. God—Fatherhood. I. Gangel, Jeffrey, 1960- II. Title.
    BV4529.17 .G36 2003
    248.8′421—dc21   2002009131

To our wives,
Betty and Beth,
whose loving support
makes possible
our fathering ministry

Contents

Foreword

In our world where men easily slide into ready-made molds, the nobility of fatherhood has steadily faded. Macho men, remote mousy geeks, or even "fun dads" pinch-hit for one of the most sobering assignments in life. Effective fatherhood is often skewed by faulty role models or misinformation, and no help at all is available for many. Our twenty-first century has quietly demoted fatherhood to a low priority with caricatures of a quasi-comic house servant whose job is to ensure that mom and the kids are well fed, well dressed, and sufficiently entertained.

What is a father's function? When a man marries a wife and children are born to them, what does God expect? Fatherhood may be a do-it-yourself pursuit, lived uniquely in each family, but God the Father has carefully modeled basic principles for that determinative role.

Kenn Gangel, my good friend and former colleague, together with his son, Jeff, has backlighted this most difficult challenge with encouragement and biblical instruction. Not only does God care about the upcoming heritage, but he is deeply concerned about developing men of reliable strength and firm character who will produce the next generation, embodying divine oversight and gentle understanding.

This father/son team has crafted a well-balanced examination of family leadership. When God created Adam *after his own likeness,* he set the standard for all father/son relationships. When Adam failed, the Father reached out in compassion and provision for his needs. Down through the centuries his faithfulness has been evident in every generation.

Fatherhood implies a commission for lifelong, multitask nurturing, demanding the highest levels of excellence. What incredible incentive—he never calls us to any task without providing the resources with which to fulfill it!

Howard G. Hendricks
Distinguished Professor
Chairman, Center for Christian Leadership
Dallas Theological Seminary

Preface

"Man," says Frederick Buechner, "is so the universe will have something to talk through, so God will have something to talk with, and so the rest of us will have something to talk about." We hope this book will accomplish all three goals: Christian dads serving as communicators of God's revelation, conversationalists with the heavenly Father, and commendable examples of godly fathering on earth.

If we could do this by developing the stories of great fathers of the Old and New Testaments, it would be an easier task. However, it would also be a very short book. The Bible shows us more failure than success in the foibles of its human fathers, even though the failure of fathers to reflect God's character often distorts a child's view of God himself. We will pick up on these negative examples to show how God builds from our weakness to his strength as we learn to function in our premier calling.

While strolling through a mall bookstore, we noticed a Father's Day table. The majority of the books on display focused on war or sports (booksellers must assume that's all we think about). The display even included *Cooking for Dummies* as a not-so-subtle gibe. Ironically, the majority of the relational "fathering" books were authored by women. We believe that Christian dads need to learn from God and need to hear from fathers who are living out the relationship.

Most fathering books approach the subject from the perspective of an author's experience or the framework of social psychology in which the central focus is child development. We have attempted to focus on Scripture, preferring to develop our message around God's fathering behavior grounded in his attributes, as found in the key text(s) for each chapter.

We realize the traditional family image is eroding and even shattered in our twenty-first-century culture. Forty percent of the children in America grow up without a father in the home. More than 250,000 children are raised by their grandparents. Television images of fathering are insulting at best and destructive at worst, rather than instructive. But we believe that God's grace and truth can equip any dad and heal any home.

Neither of us plays much golf. It's a great game, but we just find it difficult to carve out the time or cough up the bucks. Yet we do own golf clubs. In fact we both have more clubs than we can carry, stashed here and there in garages and storage rooms. As you may know, unused golf clubs not only gather dust, they tend to rust. And golf clubs are not really useful for anything other than, well, golf! Like many things in life, golf clubs are made to be used.

We hope and pray that Christian dads will use this book. Realizing that the best books are not just ones that speak to you but ones you talk about, we have included some features that will help you talk it out and work it out:

Jeff's story and Kenn's story. These personal stories in each chapter will help you see how we have struggled through our attempts to apply the attributes of God to our fathering relationships.

Making it work. In this section we try to offer some specific principles, applications, and action steps. This is where the rubber of revelation meets the road of response.

Questions for discussion. We suggest that you work through this book with a few other dads. Most men don't lack ability, they lack accountability. These questions should spur some insightful discussions for a small group and will help you personalize the principles. At the very least, use the questions for your own contemplation.

Father/child dialogue. If you really want the most from this book, share the experience with your children. You could have teenage children read the book with you and then focus together on the dialogue questions. With younger children, just take the time to share your thoughts and ask them the questions found in this section.

Whatever you do, don't let these fathering principles rust in the garage. Take them out on the links of life and play through. Fore!

one

Make 'Em Laugh

Attribute: Humor
Text: Psalm 68:3
Characters: Jacob and Family

A man with a sense of humor doesn't make jokes out of life; he merely recognizes the ones that are there.

Nuggets

One Sunday a young child began acting up during the morning worship service. The parents did their best to maintain some sense of order in the pew, but it seemed to be a losing battle. Finally, the father picked up the little guy and walked sternly up the aisle on his way out of the auditorium. Just before reaching the foyer doors, the son called out loudly to the congregation, "Pray for me! Pray for me!"

Even the most serious moments in parenting can erupt in laughter when kids are involved. Please allow yourself to smile through this chapter, because dads must learn not to take themselves too seriously. We fully believe that God intended parenting to be the most enjoyable and heartwarming job in the world. Actually let's take it a step further. God wants us to have fun fathering, because he has always fathered his children with a sense of humor and with a desire to see their lives filled with his joy.

God's Sense of Humor

God's humor permeates the story line of Scripture, especially in his dealings with his Israelite children. It begins with the father of that nation, Abraham. Can't you see the smile on God's face when he says to this ninety-nine-year-old man with a barren wife and no children, "You will be the father of many nations" (Gen. 17:4)? Abraham certainly saw the humor in this: "Abraham fell facedown; he laughed and said to himself, 'Will a son be born to a man a hundred years old? Will Sarah bear a child at the age of ninety?'" (v. 17). God answered, probably with a chuckle, "Yes!" And just to make sure that Abraham and Sarah caught the humor of it all, God said "call him Isaac" (v. 19), a name that means "he laughs." God started his Israelite family with a big round of laughter.

Years later when Abraham's little family had grown into a great nation in Egypt, God delivered them from slavery and began to lead them to their own homeland. We see some more subtle humor in the way God deals with his grumbling children. Shortly after the amazing Red Sea miracle, the people complained about the lack of food (Exodus 16). God could have provided food for them in some plain, boring way. But perhaps just to lighten the stress of their wilderness journey, God responded creatively. He rained the bread down on them! What fun! The Father provided a grand scale Easter egg hunt.

Even God's discipline comes laced with humor. The children of Israel were told not to keep the manna until morning but to gather only what they could use. "Some of them paid no attention to Moses; they kept part of it until morning, but it was full of maggots and began to smell" (v. 20). What an appropriate and humorous form of punishment.

God used a number of surprising and flat-out funny ways to protect his children, but perhaps no story evokes a smile like that of Balaam and his donkey (Num. 22:21–33). As a prophet Balaam's job was to instruct and encourage the people. As the enemies of God's people, the Moabites tried to persuade Balaam to curse Israel. On his trip to meet the Moabites, Balaam ran into but could not see the angel of the Lord on the path. His donkey could see the angel with a drawn sword, and the donkey refused to move, despite Balaam's repeated abuse. Finally, God chose to intervene in a most hilarious way. Remember, this is not Dr. Doolittle here, this is a prophet! God opened the donkey's mouth, and she spoke to Balaam. What's even more outrageous is that Balaam talked back! Check out this amazing conversation:

> Donkey: "What have I done to you to make you beat me these three times?"
> Balaam: "You have made a fool of me!" (Actually Balaam did that himself.) "If I had a sword in my hand, I would kill you right now."
> Donkey: "Am I not your own donkey, which you have always ridden, to this day? Have I been in the habit of doing this to you?"
> Balaam: "No."

Well, God opened Balaam's eyes so that he could see the angel, and Balaam ended up blessing the children of Israel instead of cursing them. Do you think God's sense of humor sometimes influences the way he teaches his children? Have you ever considered injecting some humor into your patterns of discipline and instruction with your children?

God's Joyful Family

God does not always act in humorous ways, but he does want his children to experience joy and happiness in living with him. The psalmists understood this. David says, "May the righteous be glad and rejoice before God; may they be happy and joyful" (Ps. 68:3). David even found joy in offering sacrifices: "At his tabernacle will I sacrifice with shouts of joy" (Ps. 27:6). And perhaps the children of Israel expressed their greatest joy when God brought them back from captivity.

> When the LORD brought back the captives to Zion,
>   we were like men who dreamed.
> Our mouths were filled with laughter,
>   our tongues with songs of joy.
>
> Psalm 126:1–2

If God acts to fill his spiritual family with laughter and joy, shouldn't earthly fathers plan and purpose to bring such qualities to their physical families? And if joy is such a hot commodity that it fills the words of the psalms, shouldn't we try to integrate some of that spiritual joy into the lives of our children? So who has done that effectively? Not many, apparently, because you will have difficulty finding a father in the Bible who expressed spiritual humor and joy to his children. But we do have an example of what can happen if we allow sadness and bitterness to steal that joy.

Jacob's Sad Story

Jacob, the son of Isaac, grandson of Abraham, was the father of twelve sons. God changed his name to Israel, a name that stuck for the whole nation. Now think of the fun a father could have with twelve sons. Jacob had a ready-made football or soccer team with a sub to spare. He could have watched them play five-on-five basketball with a sub on each team. Or perhaps more in keeping with their line of work, Jacob could have sponsored his own rodeo! But the words *fun* and *joy* do not appear in the biblical text describing this family.

Unfortunately, Jacob made a critical mistake in his fathering approach. "Now Israel loved Joseph more than any of his other sons, because he had been born to him in his old age; and he made a richly ornamented robe for him" (Gen. 37:3). Jacob showed favoritism. That sin bred a household filled with bitterness and hate. "When his brothers saw that their father loved him more than any of them, they hated him and could not speak a kind word to him" (v. 4).

All hope for humor in this house drains away as we see a dangerous pattern emerge. Joseph tattled on his brothers; the brothers got mad. Joseph had a dream; his brothers hated him all the more. Joseph dreamed again, and his brothers grew jealous of him. Finally, all this hatred came to a head when the brothers got their chance with Joseph out in the fields away from the protection of his father. They sold him as a slave to a caravan of Ishmaelites on their way to Egypt. Then they led their father to believe that Joseph had been killed by a wild animal.

The loss of a son is no laughing matter. But because he so favored Joseph, Jacob allowed this apparent loss to cloud his relationships with his remaining children. Notice his response: "Then Jacob tore his clothes, put on sackcloth and mourned for his son many days. All his sons and daughters came to comfort him, but he refused to be comforted. 'No,' he said, 'in mourning will I go down to the grave to my son.' So his father wept for him" (vv. 34–35). A deep fog of sadness and bitterness descended on this household, and father Jacob wrapped himself in it and would not let go.

Even years later when Joseph's brothers journeyed to Egypt to get food, Jacob had not yet dispelled the clouds of sadness from his family. On their first visit, the brothers had been instructed by Joseph to bring young Benjamin when they returned. But the idea did not sit well with Jacob, "My son will not go down there with you; his brother is dead and he is the only one left. If harm comes to him on the journey you are taking, you will bring my gray head down to the grave in sorrow" (42:38). Jacob's words drip with pessimism and despair. This was not a happy family.

Thankfully, God restored joy to this family by reuniting them in Egypt. As we know and as Joseph realized, all this had been part of God's plan to save his people (45:5–7). True joy and happiness in our families come as we trust God's plan and provision through everything.

Our Humorous Home Life

How can we fathers inject a healthy measure of humor and joy into our family life? Not every dad can play the role of stand-up comedian, and our jokes may draw more tears than laughs. Many fathers face such pressures at work that joy has been squeezed out and humor dried up. If your family has fractured in some way, then laughter may seem like a lost art. But if God truly desires us to "be joyful always" (1 Thess. 5:16), then he can supply the joy in even the toughest cases. Consider a few basic principles:

Be with Your Kids

One of the best ways for fathers to connect with their children is to intentionally enter their world. Find out what life is like for your children. Take them out to lunch, run around with them at soccer practice, help with a school project, shop at Wal-Mart together. Try joining them in even the simple and mundane tasks of life—like brushing your teeth together (your kids would love to see you with a mouthful of foam). Learn firsthand the joys and struggles that confront your children every day. Then you will better know how to encourage and humor them.

The more time you spend with your children, the more opportunities you will have to see what brings them joy. The more you see them smile, the more you will want to make them smile. And as you enter their world, let them also venture into yours. Look for ways to include your children in your daily life and routine. Let them see what life is like for you.

Back in the 1980s, Nick Stinnett conducted research on some three thousand families and drew out six main qualities that exist in strong families. The book *Family Building* grew out of that research and provides information on how to develop those qualities in the home. Though we could think of dozens of qualities that might surface on such a list, this simple principle of spending time together made the top six. In the book, psychiatrists Frank Minirth and Paul Meier explain, "There are many demands from work, school, church and extra-curricular activities that would rob us of that time and fragment us from one another. However, a child's birthright is the right to spend time with his parents."[1]

Vacations can provide some of the best opportunities for us to be with our kids. During the '60s and '70s, the Gangel family rolled across the United States each summer for five or six weeks. Kenn spoke at conferences and the rest of the family came along for the ride and the fun. Living, sleeping, driving, eating, and playing together for weeks at a time produced some of our greatest family memories.

Not all families can hit the road for weeks, but even brief getaways can create space for family fun and relationship building. But this principle must be applied to vacation time as well—

be with your kids. Family unity will not develop if Dad plays golf while Mom shops and the kids play video games.

The apostle Peter spells it out for us as he discusses relating to our wives, "Husbands, in the same way be considerate as you live with your wives" (1 Peter 3:7). We must be considerate in the way we live with our children as well, and that means we must plan to spend time with them.

Play with Your Kids

Jeff was spending a day at a water park with his kids, body-surfing in the wave pool. At the end of one wave, he nearly plowed into another playful dad who said, "Hey, Dad, we're not supposed to be having this much fun!" To that we say, "Oh, yes we are!"

The words *dad* and *work* sometimes seem synonymous, especially to children. Erma Bombeck described her childhood view of Dad: "Whenever I played house, the mother doll had a lot to do. I never knew what to do with the daddy doll, so I had him say, 'I'm going off to work now,' and threw him under the bed."[2]

If we could change an old cliché we would say, "All work and no play turns a child away." It's true that play will not put bread on the table (unless you are a professional athlete), but play satisfies our children even more than bread.

Many adults lose the art of play in the hustle and bustle of adulthood. But a little concerted effort can revive the sense of childlike imagination and the joy of play. It begins with the most simple games like peek-a-boo and hide-and-seek. A two-generation Gangel favorite requires only some floor space and willing bodies. Just expect that father/child wrestling matches will bring Mom to the doorway, saying, "Somebody's going to get hurt!" She's usually right, of course, but dads must be willing to suffer those sore backs and scraped noses for the sake of playtime. To make a child happy, no toy in the world can take the place of a dad on the floor.

Crawling-on-the-floor games usually progress to safer on-the-table games as kids grow up. Actually, table games like Pictionary and Guesstures have left our family rolling on the floor in laughter. Do you know what games your children enjoy?

Would you be willing to give up a favorite television program or football game to see your children smile?

As our children grow, we often add sports to the games. Now things get dangerous again! Dad-shaped bodies often resist the physical strain of competitive sports. Sometimes the feet won't move as fast as the head tells them to or the arms won't do what the head says they should. But children appreciate any sincere effort to join them in their sports world.

Jeff learned nearly every sport but lacrosse and rugby from Kenn. No one would ever label us athletes, but we sure know how to play together. Just watching sports has become a family event for us. Dad, if you love sports, have the patience to let your children into that arena of your life. Explain the value of the game, teach them the rules, and then take the time to play the sport at their level.

Laugh with Your Kids

Please notice we did not say to laugh *at* your kids. TV sitcoms rely on rude, cutting humor to evoke audience laughter. This should not be the case in Christian homes. We are talking about giving your children something to laugh about and then laughing with them.

In his wonderful book *Laugh Again*, Chuck Swindoll emphasizes the need for laughter in our lives, "In many homes—dare I say most?—laughter has left. Joy that was once a vital ingredient in family life has departed, leaving hearts that seldom sing, lips that rarely smile, eyes that no longer dance, and faces that say no."[3]

God never promised that family life would always be a barrel of laughs. In fact the day sin entered our world, God promised pain, sweat, and tears (Gen. 3:17–19). Sometimes the sounds of weeping and mourning fill our homes, but the writer of Ecclesiastes reminds us that we will also experience times of laughing and dancing (Eccles. 3:4). The times of mourning come without any effort. As dads, shouldn't we attempt to create more times of laughing?

It doesn't take much effort to make most children laugh. A funny face, a silly song, a crazy story, or a wacky voice can paint a wide smile on any child. Laughter can tear down the barriers of stress and conflict while building a bridge of shared joy. Try it, Dad. Don't wait for joy to come knocking on your family's door; bring it home with you and give it to those who love you most.

———∞∞∞———

Jeff's Story

I believe that God gives us children to restore our sense of humor. The joy we tend to lose in adulthood comes back to us wrapped in diapers! Just think of all the funny smells and sounds and looks that children offer. What my wife and I have treasured most are the funny words that tend to come out of our children's mouths. Here are a few examples that we have recorded.

As a toddler, Lyndsey had a terrible fear of our "backinator" (vacuum cleaner). When the machine fired up, she would tear into the living room and climb to safety on a chair. At breakfast, she talked to her Cheerios, saying, "Come here, guys!" to the few remaining Os in the milk. When they weren't eating Cheerios, our kids had "Floot Lopes" or "Flosted Flakes." The first time Lyndsey saw refried beans she asked, "Why are we eating this dog food?" And what do we have for lunch? Why, a "tune-up" sandwich of course!

My kids even made me laugh about sports. Lyndsey loved to watch "Emma Emma Gucci" (Kristi Yamaguchi). Brad loved to play "garf" (golf). But singing usually evoked the most laughter. Perhaps you know this song, "I've got the pizza pan of thunderstanding down in my heart!" What? Or how about the song about the lame man healed by Jesus, "He went whopping and weeping and praising God" (instead of walking and leaping). And Jesus' words in the same song, "In the name of Jesus Christ of Nazareth, wise up and walk." I like it! Why was Jesus born on Christmas day? "To save us all from Santa's power." Why didn't Charles Wesley think of that?

I've only begun with the stories, but you get the idea. I'm laughing right now remembering the time Bradley saw a man with a Mohawk haircut and said, "That guy has a hammock on his head!" If your children don't make you laugh, you're not listening well enough.

Kenn's Story

I completely agree—our grandchildren are as hilarious as their parents! Someone once said, "Insanity is hereditary—you catch it from your children." Perhaps. But the joy and humor this chapter extols comes from the other direction. Dour, sour, glowering fathers don't produce loving, laughing, lighthearted offspring.

A family is like a botanical garden in which tender young plants not only survive but thrive. The joy and mirth dads create in the climate of the home make possible genuine delight in their children's lives. I offer one simple example from the Gangel family.

Music has always been important, indeed essential, for all of us. I sing with a symphony chorale, Jeff in a faculty quartet. We sing duets from time to time. Lyndsey plays piano and flute; Brad takes piano and guitar lessons; Julie sings soprano in a worship team, and one of her boys attends an annual music camp.

We find in music a perfect way to worship, serve, encourage each other, and express our corporate delight in the Lord. We sing in church; we sing at home; we sing before meals; we sing after meals. It's a sacrifice of praise to the God of humor and joy.

Making It Work

"Rejoice in the Lord always. I will say it again: Rejoice!" (Phil. 4:4). Though shackled in a Roman prison, Paul had joy. And he encouraged others to find joy in Christ too. As the spiritual leader of your home, you can do the same. Don't laugh off these suggestions:

- If your joy has disappeared and you find yourself in a state of deep discouragement or depression, please seek godly counsel from a pastor or Christian counselor.
- If the smiles and laughter of God's joy have just fallen prey to the tyranny of busyness and work, then reevaluate your priorities and ask God to restore your sense of humor.

- If you appreciate the value of humor in the home but have simply neglected to jump-start that joy, then go home and wrestle with your kids or find a funny story to read to them.

- If you regularly inject your children with a strong dose of loving laughter, then thank God for his joy and pass it on to another family that may need the encouragement.

We close this chapter with a humorous retelling of the parable of the prodigal son. This creative effort appeared on the Internet as an anonymous piece.

The Prodigal Son in the Key of F

Feeling footloose and frisky, a featherbrained fellow forced his father to fork over his farthings. Fast he flew to foreign fields and frittered his family's fortune, feasting fabulously with floozies and faithless friends. Flooded with flattery he financed a full-fledged fling of "funny foam" and fast food.

Fleeced by his fellows in folly, facing famine, and feeling faintly fuzzy, he found himself a feed-flinger in a filthy foreign farmyard. Feeling frail and fairly famished, he fain would have filled his frame with foraged food from the fodder fragments.

"Fooey," he figured, "my father's flunkies fare far fancier," the frazzled fugitive fumed feverishly, facing the facts. Finally, frustrated from failure and filled with foreboding (but following his feelings) he fled from the filthy foreign farmyard.

Faraway, the father focused on the fretful form in the field and flew to him and fondly flung his forearms around the fatigued fugitive. Falling at his father's feet, the fugitive floundered forlornly, "Father, I have flunked and fruitlessly forfeited family favor."

Finally, the faithful father, forbidding and forestalling further flinching, frantically flagged the flunkies to fetch forth the finest fatling and fix a feast.

Faithfully, the father's firstborn was in a fertile field fixing fences while father and fugitive were feeling festive. The foreman felt fantastic as he flashed the fortunate news of a familiar family face that had forsaken fatal foolishness. Forty-four feet from the farmhouse the firstborn found a farmhand fixing a fatling.

Frowning and finding fault, he found father and fumed, "Floozies and foam from frittered family funds and you fix a feast following the fugitive's folderol?" The firstborn's fury flashed, but fussing was futile. The frugal firstborn felt it was fitting to feel "favored" for his faithfulness and fidelity to family, father, and farm. In foolhardy fashion, he faulted the father for failing to furnish a fatling and feast for his friends. His folly was not in feeling fit for feast and fatling for friends; rather his flaw was in his feeling about the fairness of the festival for the found fugitive. His fundamental fallacy was a fixation on favoritism, not forgiveness. Any focus on feeling "favored" will fester and friction will force the frayed façade to fall. Frankly, the father felt the frigid first-born's frugality of forgiveness was formidable and frightful. But the father's former faithful fortitude and fearless forbearance to forgive both fugitive and first-born flourishes.

The farsighted father figured, "Such fidelity is fine, but what forbids fervent festivity for the fugitive that is found? Unfurl the flags and finery, let fun and frolic freely flow. Former failure is forgotten; folly is forsaken. Forgiveness forms the foundation for future fortune."

Jesus has left us a picture of the loving father who parties when we return to him.

Questions for Discussion

1. Can you think of any other times in the Bible when God dealt humorously with his children?
2. How might you interject some joy and humor into the training and discipline of your children?
3. Why did Jacob's family have so little joy?
4. Discuss some specific ways you play and laugh with your children.

Father/Child Dialogue

1. Dad, tell your kids some funny stories from your childhood. What made you laugh back then? What gives you the most joy now?
2. Kids, tell your dad what makes you laugh. Talk about the most fun you've had with your dad. Is there something fun you would like to do with your dad? Tell him!

two

An Officer or a Gentleman?

Attributes: Grace and Mercy
Text: Nehemiah 9:16–17
Characters: Saul and Jonathan

Be merciful, just as your Father is merciful.

Luke 6:36

If fathers had been around when God was creating humankind, we could have given him a great idea. In some way, shape, or form, God should have created children with built-in Velcro strips. That way parents could just stick things to them that always tend to get lost, left behind, and forgotten—things like jackets, Bibles, and watches or schoolbooks, permission slips, and lunch money. Wouldn't it be great if kids never left anything behind?

Since we cannot produce Velcro children, fathers must deal with the need for mercy. Consider this situation. The son left his watch at the pond and it was gone forever. What's a father to do? Frustration says, "I told you a million times not to leave things lying around! No more watches for you for the rest of your life!" Justice says, "I'm sorry, son. You must learn to take

responsibility for your possessions. I know you are only eleven, but from now on you have to pay your own way around here."
But a few other voices whisper too. Mercy says, "Yes, he may deserve punishment for his negligence, but this eleven-year-old child is still learning responsibility. Give him a break!" Grace says, "Give him more than a break, give him an undeserved gift. He's already heartbroken over losing the watch; give him another watch and another chance to prove himself responsible." Mercy relents from deserved punishment or consequences. Grace offers undeserved favor or benefit.
In this particular case, mercy and grace spoke loudest. The son received a new watch wrapped in a healthy reminder about personal responsibility.

A Gracious Father

On their return from captivity in Babylon, the Israelites faced some major rebuilding projects—and not just walls and structures. The people of God had to rebuild their relationship with God. Ezra and Nehemiah led the people through a process of confession and recommitment. In so doing, they acknowledged the sins of their forefathers and thanked God for his grace and mercy. Listen to some of their words:

> But they, our forefathers, became arrogant and stiff-necked, and did not obey your commands. They refused to listen and failed to remember the miracles you performed among them. They became stiff-necked and in their rebellion appointed a leader in order to return to their slavery. But you are a forgiving God, gracious and compassionate, slow to anger and abounding in love. Therefore you did not desert them.
>
> Nehemiah 9:16–17

This statement about God's gracious character rings loud and often throughout the pages of the Old Testament (Exod. 34:6; Deut. 4:31; 2 Chron. 30:9; Ps. 25:6; 103:8; Dan. 9:9; Jonah 4:2). God's dealings with his unfaithful nation provide us with a dramatic picture of his grace and mercy. Over and over again the Israelites forgot him, failed him, and forsook him. Countless times they rebelled against God's law, squandered his blessings, and deserved his judgment. Yet God never deserted them. He never broke his covenant with them. He never allowed his righteous anger to submerge his mercy or bury his grace. He remained gracious and compassionate, slow to anger, and abounding in love. He did not always mete out the punishment his children deserved, and he often blessed them in ways they did not deserve.

As human fathers, our tempers can sometimes drown out the voices of mercy and grace. Consider, for instance, one famous angry father.

An Angry Father

Saul, the first king of Israel, the leader of God's people, was Jonathan's father. God had made Saul king, but Saul struggled with jealousy and insecurity, especially when David came along. As the women sang, "Saul has slain his thousands, and David his tens of thousands," Saul began murmuring a refrain of jealousy and anger against David (see 1 Sam. 18:5–16).

Jealous anger turned to death threats, and David confided in his friend Jonathan, the king's own son. Because of their close friendship, Jonathan vowed to discover the depth of his father's hatred for David. So when David did not show up for family meals two days in a row, Jonathan stood up for him and offered an explanation. The fury of Saul's jealous heart lashed out at his own son (20:30–33).

Saul loved his son Jonathan. He wanted Jonathan to have the throne and the kingdom. But his obsession over kingship led to his jealousy of David and anger against his own son. Unwilling to show any grace or mercy toward David, Saul ended up keeping it from Jonathan as well. Driven by his own passions, Saul lost perspective. He failed to do what was best for the kingdom. He failed to appreciate the friendship between Jonathan and David. He failed to dispense mercy and grace. And he failed to be a gracious father.

Saul's stubbornness also squelched his ability to show mercy and grace. Even earlier in his career, Saul allowed his stubborn heart to cloud his fatherly grace. In the midst of a heated battle against the Philistines, Saul made a rash oath. He bound his army by saying, "Cursed be any man who eats food before evening comes, before I have avenged myself on my enemies!" (14:24). But Jonathan missed the meeting and had not heard his father's oath. He ate some honey that day, innocently violating the decree. When God would not respond to Saul's inquiry, he used lots to discover who had disobeyed. And sure enough, the lot fell on Jonathan. Saul said, "May God deal with me, be it ever so severely, if you do not die, Jonathan" (v. 44).

What a natural opportunity for mercy! Jonathan had innocently broken the decree. He had been a hero in the battle. And Saul should have admitted his mistake in uttering the curse in the first place. But the king stuck to his stubborn guns, and in his pride refused mercy to his own son. The army had to step in: "But the men said to Saul, 'Should Jonathan die—he who has brought about this great deliverance in Israel? Never! As surely as the Lord lives, not a hair of his head will fall to the ground, for he did this today with God's help.' So the men rescued Jonathan, and he was not put to death" (v. 45).

Saul displays a common male problem—his will became the standard for his actions. He would bend the rules when it served his own purposes (see 15:7–11) and then try to enforce his own ill-conceived rule when he wanted to protect his authority, even if it meant his own son would suffer. Once he strayed from God's absolute standard of right and wrong, Saul left no room for grace and mercy.

In his book *Unfinished Business,* our friend Charles Sell tells about a father who failed to understand the importance of grace and mercy in relating to his son.

> In his men's seminar, David Simmons, a former cornerback for the Dallas Cowboys, tells about his childhood home. His father, a military man, was extremely demanding, rarely saying a kind word, always pushing him with harsh criticism to do better. The father had decided that he would never permit his son to feel any satisfaction from his accomplishments, reminding him there were always new goals ahead. When Dave was a little boy, his dad gave him a bicycle, unassembled, with the command that he put it together. After Dave struggled to the point of tears with the difficult instructions and many parts, his father said, "I knew you

couldn't do it." Then he assembled it for him. When Dave played football in high school, his father was unrelenting in his criticisms. In the backyard of his home, after every game, his dad would go over every play and point out Dave's errors. "Most boys got butterflies in the stomach before the game; I got them afterwards. Facing my father was more stressful than facing any opposing team."[1]

God does not act like a military commander; he treats us like a gracious Father. God doesn't set a legalistic standard; he sets a holy standard. Legalism stands harsh, strict, and unbending. Holiness recognizes weaknesses, deals with sin, and works for growth. Legalism seeks to crush people with the standard. Holiness seeks to call people to the standard.

A Merciful Father

So, Dad, does legalism mark your fathering? Do you focus more on rules than righteousness? Are you more likely to threaten murder than to offer mercy? Do you always opt for grounding rather than grace? Such oppressive parenting douses the spark in children and, as the Bible says, can discourage or provoke them (Eph. 6:4; Col. 3:21).

God is not soft on sin, but, for his children, God desires holiness not legal perfection. Instead of getting us to "toe the line," God prefers to bring us to the point at which we allow him to carry us along. Like God, we cannot be soft on the sin in our children, but we must be gracious and merciful in the way we "bring them up in the training and instruction of the Lord" (Eph. 6:4). Discipline, by nature, involves giving tender direction not harsh correction.

But what about the other extreme? Can we be too merciful and gracious? Yes! We call it "license." But the problem is not in the amount of grace or mercy. When we extend mercy and grace in a context of righteousness, holiness, and justice, they will not become license. When mercy and grace become spiritual labels for letting a child get away with sin, that creates license. Grace and mercy must exist in balance with justice and discipline.

Consider this example from the ministry of Jesus in John 8. As Jesus taught people in the temple courts, some teachers of the law and the Pharisees interrupted him with one of their planned traps. They shoved a humiliated woman to the front of the crowd and said, "Teacher, this woman was caught in the act of adultery. In the Law Moses commanded us to stone such women. Now what do you say?" (vv. 4–5). This trap directly challenged Jesus' message of mercy and forgiveness. Would he defy the very law of Moses? Then they could accuse him of heresy. Would he let them stone her? That would compromise his stand for mercy. The religious leaders thought they had Jesus between a rock and a hard place, between legalism and license, with no other options.

Jesus let them squirm a little in their own trap. He bent down and wrote in the sand while they waited for his answer. When he stood up, he surprised everyone. "If any one of you is without sin, let him be the first to throw a stone at her" (v. 7). Then he went back to his sandpainting. And here the apostle John provides us with a fascinating sidelight: "At this, those who heard began to go away one at a time, the older ones first" (v. 9). The wiser ones among them recognized the acute wisdom in Jesus' response.

Legalism, living by the law, cannot be applied by certain people in certain situations. He who enforces the law on others will come under the law himself. Only someone sinless could perfectly enforce the law. Ironically, Jesus was the only person in that crowd who had the right to throw a stone! Yet he chose to offer mercy instead, mercy that also addressed the sin issue. Notice that the story does not end with the stone throwers' departure.

"Jesus straightened up and asked her, 'Woman, where are they? Has no one condemned you?' 'No one, sir,' she said. 'Then neither do I condemn you,' Jesus declared. 'Go now and leave your life of sin'" (vv. 10–11). Mercy—Jesus did not throw the stone she deserved. Grace—Jesus offered her the chance to change her ways. But he did not do so without challenging, even commanding, her to leave her life of sin. Jesus struck the perfect balance between the rock of legalism and the hard place of license. He gently set this woman in the soft spot of God's mercy and grace.

Fathers, we must follow this example. We must find that soft balance. Legalism can strangle the spiritual life right out of our

children. License will open the floodgates of spiritual immoral-
ity. Only mercy and grace deal with sin as God does. Instead of
condemning, we forgive and we help our children along the path
to holiness.

⸙

Jeff's Story

I can honestly say that my dad did a masterful job of dispensing
the right amount of mercy and grace at just the right time. During one of my summers at home during college years, my car fell
ill and I borrowed my dad's car to get to and from work while he
was out of town. One day I was in such a hurry to get home that
I began tailgating the car in front of me. And sure enough, when
that car stopped suddenly, I could not stop fast enough. Before
I knew it, I was sitting on the side of the road staring at the front
of my dad's car. The hood looked more like an A-frame roof! The
grill had splintered into tiny pieces. I drove home devastated and
more than just a little fearful of what my dad might say!

I intended to have the damage repaired before he came home
a few days later. I found a body repair shop and paid the
deductible. Then I waited for Dad's return. I knew that I had to
tell him, but the shame brought fear to the task. When Dad came
home, he listened politely to my sob story, he nodded knowingly,
and he accepted my explanation graciously. He wasn't even
upset! He saw that I had learned some valuable lessons, that I
had already paid the consequences for my mistake, and by his
very attitude and response, he extended mercy and grace to me.

Kenn's Story

During more than forty years of preaching and teaching,
many people have asked me what theme or topic excites me
most. To put it another way, if God restricted me to only one
sermon for the rest of my life, what would I say? The question
poses no challenge. I choose the grace of God.

Too often we limit our discussions of grace to *saving grace,* the work of God that gives us redemption through Jesus' death on the cross. But every dad knows that *serving grace* and *parenting grace* make possible the family ministry to which God has called us. Actually, everything in our lives depends on his grace— from the air we breathe to the most complex tasks at work or the most painful demands of parenting.

Making It Work

Dads, our heavenly Father is merciful with us. Let's look for opportunities to extend his mercy and grace to our children! You can begin with a few of these ideas:

- Acknowledge and celebrate God's mercy and grace at work in your own life. Talk about it with your family and testify to it when you are with others.
- When you deal with sin and disobedience in your children, don't just react. Think through the extremes of legalism and license. Consider the response that would be too harsh and the one that would be too permissive. Then choose the solid middle ground of mercy and grace.
- Pray daily that God will help you develop holiness in your children as you recognize their weaknesses, deal with their sin, and move them toward spiritual growth.

As we seek to imitate our gracious and merciful Father, let's have the patience of Jesus to draw in the sand and not react to situations with the rash words of a Saul. Let's temper our tempers with a solid dose of God's mercy. And let's ask God to Velcro his grace to our hearts so that we never lose that perspective.

Questions for Discussion

1. Talk about some examples of God's mercy and grace in his relationship with the children of Israel.

2. What factors/issues in Saul's life squelched his ability to show mercy and grace?
3. When does legalism most often rear its ugly head in our fathering?
4. When does license most often become the easy way out for fathers?
5. Talk about a John 8 type of situation in which your child was caught in some sin. How did you deal with it? How could you have struck a better balance between legalism and license in that situation?

Father/Child Dialogue

1. Dad, explain to your children the difference between mercy and grace. Use an example or two from your own family life.
2. Kids, talk to your dad about rules and punishment in your family. Do you feel the rules are too strict or the punishment too harsh? Explain why or why not.

three

Focus on the Father

Attribute: Forgiveness
Text: Luke 15:11–32
Characters: Father and Prodigal Sons

> His heart was as great as the world, but there was no room in it to hold the memory of wrong.
>
> Ralph Waldo Emerson

The tears flowed like water through a downspout. Bradley struggled with the weight of guilt and the desire to maintain self-righteousness. It was not a "big" sin. He and his sister had decided to play at the soccer field for an hour beyond the usual soccer practice time. The field was walking distance from home, and there was no real danger or malice in their decision, except that they had not asked or informed Mom and Dad! As they played, supper cooled and parents stewed.

When they arrived home an hour late, the excuses poured forth. "We thought you knew where we were!" A lame excuse to be sure, but a demonstration of the sinful nature's attempt to deflect guilt and avoid those gut-wrenching words, "I was wrong."

As he lay in bed that night, Bradley faced the overwhelming prospect of needing to apologize to his parents and seek their forgiveness. Eventually, the tears softened his resolve and the

"I'm sorry" spilled out. His parents, nearly in tears themselves, bathed Brad in forgiveness.

The Father in Heaven

Forgiveness is one of God's characteristics for which we can be deeply thankful. Because the Father has forgiven us, we can be loving fathers who minister to our own children. In Luke 15 Jesus tells a story of forgiveness without even using the word. He casts the heavenly Father in the role of an earthly father who lavishes compassion on his two sons. This story provides some dramatic glimpses into the character of our Father but also displays a challenging character sketch for every earthly father.

At first the story seems to focus on the younger son. He showed selfishness and stupidity by asking for his inheritance early. Surely surprised when his father agreed, the boy took the money and ran, heading far away to blow his wad on "wild living." In the early part of the parable we don't learn any of the details, but in verse 30 Jesus has the older brother say, "When this son of yours who has squandered your property with prostitutes comes home, you kill the fattened calf for him!" This was no spring break; it appears the boy wanted to get as far away as possible from family constraints. The "distant country" surely indicates some Gentile nation marked by pagan values and heathen behavior well out of sync with the way he had been brought up.

Using his inheritance to set up a new business or buy a new farm would have been one thing, squandering it in pagan behavior quite another. Only Christian fathers who have watched their sons walk through the ravages of sin's destruction can really relate to the extremity of this parable. Only they can imagine the hours of agony and the days of loneliness the father endured.

As the story goes, life hit the son with a double whammy—his money ran out and famine struck the land. The not-so-nice Jewish boy ended up in a despicable place—a pagan pigpen. Picture a rebellious Christian teenager, brought up on Bible memory and youth group fellowship, cleaning toilets in a bar somewhere in Las Vegas. Now imagine that you're his father. At this point the Pharisees must have smiled and perhaps murmured to each other, "Right on. Jesus has finally figured it out! Sinners should get what they deserve."

Yes, we can all see ourselves in the role of the son, running from God's love because of our own selfishness and stubbornness. But many dads have experienced the grief of watching a son turn his back on everything his parents have taught him and walk out the door.

But this was not a one-child family. The older son doesn't know it, but he needs his father's forgiveness too. While Jesus develops the character of the younger son to represent the sinners who gathered to hear his stories, the older son reflects the Pharisees standing in the background, steeped in their own self-righteousness. In the older son's eyes, he was the perfect child—obedient, faithful, and hardworking, the kind of kid that brings credit to any family.

But when the younger son returns, the true character of his older brother emerges. It turns out his obedience sprang only from duty and he hated every minute of it. In anger he says to the father, "Look! All these years I've been slaving for you and never disobeyed your orders. Yet you never gave me even a young goat so I could celebrate with my friends" (vv. 28–29). This seemingly compliant son had exactly the same sin problems as his younger brother—selfishness, disrespect for his father, and stubbornness. External civility is stripped away in this moment of crisis, and bitter contempt pours out. This kid hates his family, despises his brother, and feels victimized by the prosperity all around him. The younger son repented but, as far as the story goes, the other son never did.

The Father on the Road

In a beautiful picture of repentance we see the younger son come to his senses (demonstrating that sin is a senseless way to live). As hard as it must have been to do so, he went back to his father (not just his home) to acknowledge his sin and offer to work as a day laborer.

But as much as we like to make the younger brother the star of this story because of his seemingly courageous return, let's remember that he had no options. He is clearly the object of forgiveness in the parable; the real spotlight falls on the father. Let's not miss what the father has already done at this point. He allowed the younger son to make his own choice, even though it was clearly a bad one. He didn't chase after him, but he didn't give up on him either. He didn't fall apart but demonstrated enough faith to believe that the son would return.

In Jesus' parables often there were details that stretched his listeners' minds beyond belief. The celebration is one of those details. The most Jesus' listeners would have expected was what the son hoped for, an end to starvation and a lowly slot on the social ladder. Surely this hurt and angry father would punish his rebellious son and that would be the moral of the story. As first-century Jews understood the law, that would have been a logical and quite acceptable conclusion.

But we say again that this is a story not about justice but about forgiveness. Don't miss the timing. The text tells us that the father was filled with compassion and ran toward the son "while he was still a long way off" (v. 20), not after he heard his confession, not after he saw some genuine repentance. For the heavenly Father and Christian fathers, forgiveness is based on unconditional love and unconditional grace.

In amazement the tax collectors, sinners, and Pharisees listened to this story unfold (vv. 1–2). It didn't matter what the son had done, only that he had returned. The father didn't merely accept the son back, he reconciled him, restored him, and rejoiced in the relationship. Don't miss what Jesus says about God. The heavenly Father doesn't dole out forgiveness grudgingly. He runs to the opportunity and delights in the experience. God loves to forgive; for him it's a party. Did you hear that, fellow dads? Forgiving a repentant child offers reason for celebration!

The Father in the Barn

We've already noted the older brother's reaction to all this hoopla. But now we see the father's response to the sin of self-righteousness. Could he have ordered the older brother inside immediately? Of course, but this father does not pull rank. He personally seeks out the son and pleads with him to return. He takes the initiative and reaches out to reaffirm the older brother's place in the family and carefully explains the reason for the celebration. He changes the words of the older brother ("this son of yours") to "this brother of yours."

What a wonderful model of fathering! It doesn't matter whether his children run away or hide in the barn. It doesn't matter whether they demonstrate rebellion or bitter compliance. The forgiveness of loving fathers reaches everywhere to deal graciously with those who don't deserve it. Sometimes forgiveness can change "fight or flight" to "stay and pray." Chuck Swindoll offers five reasons why "it is best to work through rather than walk out."

- It is the continual counsel of Scripture.
- One's growth in Christ is strengthened.
- The testimony of Christ before the public is enhanced.
- "Working through" forces necessary changes. To walk out means we take our same hang-ups into the next relationship.
- Children in the family remain more secure, stable and balanced. They also learn to run if parents run . . . or work out the difficulties if that's what Mom and Dad model.[1]

Jeff's Story

I can identify somewhat with the older brother in Jesus' parable. In our family I was the compliant child and my sister, Julie, the strong-willed younger sibling. I got compliments; Julie got spankings. I pretended to sleep at nap time; Julie bounced around the bed until she got in trouble. I would pout when no one was looking; Julie would throw public temper tantrums. But our parents loved us both and treated us equally. I needed discipline just as much as Julie. And I needed forgiveness just as often too.

The path to forgiveness must cross the footbridge of equality. Christian fathers can't love one child more than the other because of behavior, personality, or circumstances. And, thank God, neither does he. (By the way, that noisy little sister is now a loving and intelligent kindergarten teacher and mother of two.)

Kenn's Story

My story is quite different. Fathered by an atheist who divorced my mother when I was ten, I grew up on a diet of anger and blasphemy with virtually no concern or love shown by my father. In fact, after the divorce, I saw my dad only once and that was when, after becoming an adult, I initiated a search to find him.

God's grace allows us to pour out on our children the love and forgiveness our parents showed us. But the same grace can enable us to demonstrate true love and forgiveness even though we may have experienced only unhappiness and fear. As a child of this Father who forgives, you too can learn to forgive.

Making It Work

Forgiveness appears on the list of those many things much easier to talk about than to do. We talk to grieving parents about forgiving children who have desperately hurt them. We often hear expressions like, "But you don't know what he did to me!" And in most cases that's true; we don't know. But the very extremes of this parable emphasize that no boundaries hem in God's forgiveness. You cannot behave so badly that you stretch the boundaries of God's grace beyond the breaking point. And because God's grace is activated in our lives through the Holy Spirit, our forgiveness can be boundless as well—as difficult and painful as that may seem.

But let's get more specific. Christ's parable provides us with some practical principles. Have a look at some guidelines for making forgiveness work with your kids.

- Have faith in your children. Don't frustrate them, don't manipulate them, and don't give up on them. If you have a wandering child, keep watching the road and expecting the heavenly Father to shepherd him home again.
- Unconditionally forgive your children. As someone has said, "If forgiveness is conditional, it isn't forgiveness at all." Wise fathers initiate reconciliation and then, when it happens, celebrate it with enthusiasm. Whatever killing the fattened calf means in your family, do it.
- Be fair with your children. Turn your back on favoritism and broken promises. Don't smile at the compliant child and frown at the rebel. Don't give too much attention to the strong-willed child and shortchange the quiet one.

This is heavy stuff, difficult, troublesome, and seemingly beyond our frail human capacity. But this parable surely intends to tell us that only in unconditional forgiveness can we reflect the heavenly Father. In that small town, not one citizen could question for a moment exactly how the father felt about the son's return. Probably both sons would have gladly agreed with the prodigal's plan to become a servant, but the father's love would not permit it. We find it exciting in this parable to discover that whatever rejoicing the prodigal may have experienced as a result of his acceptance, the joy of the father was even greater!

Questions for Discussion

1. Think about the worst possible thing one of your children could do to grieve and anger you. Now talk about how you could respond in forgiveness if that unthinkable event ever actually occurred.
2. Name some ways reconciliation has taken place in your family or church.
3. Identify at least one character trait you see in the father of this parable that you would like God to develop in your life.

Father/Child Dialogue

1. Dad, tell your kids about a time you needed and received God's forgiveness. They love to hear about your mistakes!
2. Kids, tell Dad about a time when his forgiveness meant a lot to you—and if it fits, tell him how you need his forgiveness now.

four

The Ultimate Sacrifice

Attribute: Love
Text: Exodus 34:4–7
Characters: David and Absalom

As a father has compassion on his children, so the LORD has compassion on those who fear him.

Psalm 103:13

Erma Bombeck weaves a telling tale about God's desire for loving fathers. The theology may be a bit suspect, but the heart of God seems to come through:

> When the good Lord was creating fathers he started with a tall frame. And a female angel nearby said, "What kind of father is that? If you're going to make children so close to the ground, why have you put fathers up so high? He won't be able to shoot marbles without kneeling, tuck a child in bed without bending, or even kiss a child without a lot of stooping." And God smiled and said, "Yes, but if I make him child-size, who would children have to look up to?"
>
> And when God made a father's hands, they were large and sinewy. And the angel shook her head sadly and said, "Do you know what you're doing? Large hands are clumsy. They can't manage diaper pins, small buttons, or rubber bands on pony tails, or even remove splinters caused by baseball bats." And God smiled

and said, "I know, but they're large enough to hold everything a small boy empties from his pockets at the end of a day . . . yet small enough to cup a child's face in his hands."

God worked throughout the night, giving the father few words, but a firm authoritative voice; eyes that saw everything, but remained calm and tolerant. Finally, almost as an afterthought, he added tears. Then he turned to the angel and said, "Now, are you satisfied that he can love as much as a mother?" The angel shutteth up.[1]

Yes, God has given fathers the capacity to love, and our love should mimic the love of our heavenly Father.

Perfect Love

It represented their second chance in a long list of chances. God's children had grown impatient while Moses received the law on Mount Sinai. They had worshiped a golden calf, defiled themselves, and angered Moses. The first stone tablets lay in chunks on the ground. And as God prepared to print out another copy for Moses, he described his perfect love for these children:

> So Moses chiseled out two stone tablets like the first ones and went up Mount Sinai early in the morning, as the LORD had commanded him; and he carried the two stone tablets in his hands. Then the LORD came down in the cloud and stood there with him and proclaimed his name, the LORD. And he passed in front of Moses, proclaiming, "The LORD, the LORD, the compassionate and gracious God, slow to anger, abounding in love and faithfulness, maintaining love to thousands, and forgiving wickedness, rebellion and sin. Yet he does not leave the guilty unpunished; he punishes the children and their children for the sin of the fathers to the third and fourth generation."

> Exodus 34:4–7

Even in the context of the law, God reaffirmed his love for his children, Israel. God presents his love as a two-sided coin. On the one side, God is slow to anger; he forgives wickedness, rebellion, and sin. But on the other side, God's love and faithfulness require him to punish his children when they do wrong. God's love is tender and terrible; it is gracious and just. But do not misunderstand this love. God's love is neither fickle nor moody. God's love is not unpredictable. It maintains perfect balance between grace and discipline. Our actions or emotions cannot sway God's love. His very character and being exude love.

In this passage, the Lord reintroduced himself to Moses, "The LORD, the LORD, the compassionate and gracious God." He is the very essence of love; God is love (1 John 4:8, 16). Therefore God's love is unconditional. God may express his love in various ways, but it will always be perfect love because God's character cannot change.

True fatherly love, then, must be multifaceted and unconditional. And unconditional love for sinful children requires sacrifice. To forgive sin, God had to provide a sacrifice for sin. His love required a sacrifice. "For God so loved the world that he gave his one and only Son, that whoever believes in him shall not perish but have eternal life" (John 3:16).

To love our children unconditionally, we must be willing to sacrifice. If we do not love them unconditionally, we will end up sacrificing the relationship. We've seen the mistake that King Saul made as an angry father who neglected grace and mercy. Now we observe his successor, King David, who seemed to have almost the opposite problem. His conditional, permissive love ended in the ultimate sacrifice.

Permissive Love

Undoubtedly, David served as Israel's most famous king. Perhaps even the godliest king. God himself sought out and chose this "man after his own heart" (1 Sam. 13:14). But David failed in his fathering role. He substituted permissiveness for love and it cost him two sons.

The sad story of David's fathering woes begins in 2 Samuel 13. David's son Amnon fell in love with his half sister Tamar, a full sister to Absalom, another son of David by a different wife. Such a family system already raises red flags! Well, the story goes from bad to worse. Amnon raped Tamar and then sent her away, refusing to marry her after dishonoring her. Verse 21 of chapter 13 tells us that David heard about this terrible sin and became furious. But he did nothing. And so hatred grew in Absalom's heart against his brother Amnon and possibly against his father too.

That anger stewed in Absalom's heart for two years, until he cooked up a plan to kill Amnon. Carrying out his plan, Absalom then fled. David mourned for his absent, murderous son Absalom even more than he did for dead Amnon (v. 37). And even though "the spirit of the king longed to go to Absalom" (v. 39), David would not seek reconciliation with his son until Joab finally talked him into allowing Absalom to return. Even then, David would not allow Absalom to see his face (14:23–24).

For two years this father and son lived in the same city without seeing or speaking to one another. Finally, Absalom tired of the wait. He set Joab's fields on fire to get his attention and used him to get a message to his father, "I want to see the king's face, and if I am guilty of anything, let him put me to death" (14:32). They were not exactly words of reconciliation, but they had their desired effect. David summoned Absalom to the palace. The son came in and bowed his face to the ground before the king, and David kissed him.

What a beautiful expression of love and reconciliation, right? But apparently it only represented a surface relationship. Outward gestures of love cannot take the place of true reconciliation. Since David and Absalom never resolved the issues that had come between them, the love relationship remained in shambles.

As time went on, Absalom quietly orchestrated a conspiracy against his father's rule. When he had won the hearts of the Israelites, he set up his rival rule in Hebron and proclaimed himself king. It's interesting that, as soon as David heard about it, he assumed the worst about his son. David said, "Come! We must flee, or none of us will escape from Absalom. We must leave immediately, or he will move quickly to overtake us and bring ruin upon us and put the city to the sword" (15:14). Did David know something about the heart of Absalom that he had tried to ignore?

David and the rest of his clan deserted the palace and headed to the desert. Meanwhile, Absalom took over Jerusalem and the throne. He even raped his father's concubines who had remained behind. Absalom did this to dishonor his father and to strengthen his rule over the people. Intent on killing David, Absalom gathered the armies of Israel and went out in battle against David's men.

As David's men went out, he gave orders, "Be gentle with the young man Absalom for my sake" (18:5). But the battle, which took place in the forest of Ephraim, claimed twenty thousand lives, including the life of Absalom. This angry son met one of the saddest endings recorded in the Bible. While riding his mule, his handsome, thick hair tangled in the branches of a large oak tree. Absalom hung there while his mule ran on. When Joab found him, he plunged three javelins into Absalom's heart, then threw his body into a pit and piled stones on top of him.

When the news of Absalom's death reached David, we see the sad picture of a loving father who never really knew how to *show* love to his son. David wept bitterly, "O my son Absalom! My son, my son Absalom! If only I had died instead of you—O Absalom, my son, my son!" (18:33). David mourned for the son who had murdered a brother, stolen the kingdom, dishonored the royal family, and attempted to kill his own father. David wept because he knew he had failed his son. When Joab went to David to convince him to end his mourning, he summarized David's problem with these words: "You love those who hate you and hate those who love you" (19:6). Actually David's inability to show fatherly love communicated hate and therefore had produced hatred in the heart of Absalom. David showed his love in permissiveness and sorrow rather than through unconditional sacrifice.

Proper Love

David needed to reread some of his own psalms. Godly love is not permissive love. God himself demonstrates that. "The LORD loves righteousness and justice; the earth is full of his unfailing love" (Ps. 33:5). David said, "I will sing of your love and justice; to you, O LORD, I will sing praise" (Ps. 101:1). "Deal with your servant according to your love and teach me your decrees" (Ps. 119:124). David should have known that true love sets boundaries. True love teaches right from wrong. True love upholds the need for righteousness and justice.

David failed to demonstrate such love in a number of ways. He should have loved Amnon enough to correct him and punish the sin of rape. He should have loved Absalom enough to help him work through his hatred for Amnon. He should have loved Absalom enough to correct and punish his sin of murder instead of just rejecting him. He should have loved Absalom enough to communicate with him and to seek true reconciliation. He should have loved the rest of his family enough to face Absalom and deal with his rebellion. David should have loved his children enough to stay involved in their lives and to correct their sin.

Dads, having unconditional love means that we sacrifice our own convenience to build the conscience of the child. Love does not say, "Do what you want!" Love says, "I want you to do what is right and I'll take the time to teach you!" "Love does not delight in evil but rejoices with the truth" (1 Cor. 13:6).

———— ∞ ————

Jeff's Story

You've been in this situation before. You know what I'm talking about. It's a family car ride. The kids are in the backseat. The noise level rises. A fight breaks out. Sitting in the driver's seat, I'm tempted to yell out above the fray, "Be quiet back there or I'll . . . !" But the words don't come because I don't really know what I'll do! We're already late, I can't reach back there, and my self-control has vented like smoke from my ears.

But one of the best parenting decisions Beth and I ever made was to tell our children that if they fought in the car, we would pull over. Yes, sometimes it caused us inconvenience and even embarrassment. I'm sure we looked ridiculous parked on the side of the road leaning over the front seat of our station wagon talking to our children. But we determined to love them enough to deal with their disobedience and misbehavior immediately, wherever we were. Sometimes that meant delaying an errand or walking out of church or leaving a concert. But that's what unconditional, uncompromising love does.

Kenn's Story

She died of bone cancer on September 12, 1977. For days I had lain facedown on my study floor tearfully begging God for her life. But she died. And I wasn't there—I was busy—at the office.

My mother had been pressed into service as my "dad." She became my only parent, a Swiss immigrant who never went to high school. God brought her to the cross when I was only three, and she began to literally incarnate New Testament love—especially to her only child. Everything I ever became I owe to God's grace and a single mom's sacrificial love.

There are one-parent dads out there too, many who work all day and come home to care for children. Whether you fit in that category or have a great relationship with your wife, the message is the same—love your kids generously.

Making It Work

Think of God's love as a perfectly balanced scale. On one side rests acceptance and on the other sits discipline. God accepts us despite our sin; he disciplines us because of our sin. He loves us unconditionally; he loves us sacrificially. He receives us as his beloved children; he punishes us as his beloved children. God is never so accepting that he overlooks our sin. But neither is he such a disciplinarian that he turns us away.

We cannot love our children with such perfect balance, but we can learn from God's example and adjust our "love scales" in some practical ways:

- Learn to appreciate God's unconditional, sacrificial love in your own life. Accept his forgiveness as love and receive his discipline as love.
- Beware of conditional, permissive love. Don't exasperate your children by ignoring their sin. Weak-willed fathers often produce strong-willed children. Love your children enough to expose, forgive, and correct their sin.

- Always keep God's love balance in mind. When you discipline, communicate complete acceptance. When you forgive, communicate the seriousness of sin.

In his popular book *How to Really Love Your Child,* Dr. Ross Campbell reminds us of the foundational importance of unconditional love. "We can be confident that a child is correctly disciplined only if our primary relationship with him is one of unconditional love. Without a basis of unconditional love it is not possible to understand a child, his behavior, or to know how to deal with misbehavior."[2] Campbell's book presents the expression of love in four areas: eye contact, physical touch, focused attention, and discipline.

A firm commitment to practice such tangible love in our homes will fill the "love tanks" of our children and should keep them from getting their hair caught in trees!

Questions for Discussion

1. Describe some situations in the Bible where God loved his children out of their sin and back into righteousness.
2. Why do you think David neglected to confront the sin of his children? In what ways does unconditional love require sacrifice?
3. Why does a child need eye contact, physical touch, and focused attention when receiving discipline?

Father/Child Dialogue

1. Dad, tell your children how much you love them by communicating more than just the three words "I love you." Try this leading line, "I love you enough to . . ."
2. Kids, did you know that your parents need your love too? In fact you can show your love for them through eye contact, physical touch, and focused attention. Ask your dad how you can demonstrate your love for him.

five

The Green-Eyed Monster?

Attribute: Jealousy
Text: Exodus 34:14
Characters: Hosea and Family

> I hope you will put up with a little of my foolishness. . . . I am jealous for you with a godly jealousy . . . so that I might present you as a pure virgin to [Christ].
>
> 2 Corinthians 11:1–2

Two seriously ill men in a hospital ward had been placed in a double room that was bare except for two bedside lockers. One door led into the busy hallway, and there was one window.

For an hour each day the nurses would prop up one of the men to drain fluid from his lungs. As it happened, he had the bed by the window. Total rest and quiet were necessary for both of them—no reading, no radio, no television. For hours each day they talked about their families, their jobs, their hobbies, their experiences in the military, places they had visited on vacation, and scores of other subjects.

As the man by the window (let's call him Sam) sat up each day, he described for his roommate (Bill) what he could see out the window. Bill lived for those descriptions, and they became the highlight of his day. Since the window apparently overlooked a small park with a lake, Sam would talk about children playing, lovers walking hand in hand, the trees and flowers, and the view of the city skyline just beyond the boundaries of the park. With practice, Bill could even visualize things Sam described and was grateful to see the world through the eyes of another. But one day Bill heard the description of a parade and a little peck of envy punctured his balloon of joy at receiving only secondhand reports of the world. He asked himself, *Why should Sam be the one who sees everything? Why shouldn't I have the bed by the window and a chance to look out once in a while?*

The attitude eroded his joy and took control of his mind. He went into deep moodiness and depression and, instead of recuperating, became more seriously ill.

One night over by the window, Sam began to cough and choke, shaking so violently that his hands couldn't find the nursing call button. In the next bed, Bill watched without a sound. The coughing continued in the darkness until all of a sudden it stopped—and Bill continued to stare at the ceiling.

When the morning nurse came in for baths, she found Sam dead. Quietly they removed the body. As soon as it seemed appropriate, Bill asked to be moved to the bed by the window. The nurse tucked him in and left him alone, quiet and still. As soon as she had gone, Bill struggled to prop himself up. When he had pulled the curtain back, he discovered to his dismay that the window faced a brick wall![1]

Jealousy has been aptly described as the green-eyed monster. Someone once said that there are two kinds of people in the world—those who divide the world into two groups and those who do not. One could also argue that there are two kinds of jealousy—positive and negative. We have all suffered from negative jealousy, and certainly that's the way we use the word in common conversation. However, a secondary meaning of the word tells us that to be *jealous* is to be "intolerant of rivalry or unfaithfulness." The *New Collegiate Dictionary* calls it "vigilant in guarding a possession." That explains why when we open the Bible, we see the word used to describe God.

Call Me "Jealous"

Let's begin all the way back in Exodus.

You shall not make for yourself an idol in the form of anything in heaven above or on the earth beneath or in the waters below. You shall not bow down to them or worship them; for I, the LORD your God, am a jealous God, punishing the children for the sin of the fathers to the third and fourth generation of those who hate me.

Exodus 20:4–5

Do not worship any other god, for the LORD, whose name is Jealous, is a jealous God.

Exodus 34:14

In his final charge to Israel, Joshua reminds the nation of this important point: "You are not able to serve the LORD. He is a holy God; he is a jealous God" (Josh. 24:19). What could these texts (and others like them) possibly mean? How could a God of love, mercy, and grace tell us his name is Jealous?

Exodus 20 lists the Ten Commandments, and the context has to do with idolatry. Because God is jealous for his own people, he is zealous that their love and dependence focus completely on him (Deut. 5:9; 6:15; 32:16, 21). Exodus 34 reviews God's covenant with Israel describing his complete rule over his people. He would tolerate no rivals and wanted the people to remember this by even saying his name was Jealous. These are not the words of Moses, because Exodus 34:10 begins, "Then the LORD said."

One of the great biblical metaphors for God is husband. In the New Testament this transfers to Christ and the church, but even in the Old Testament God is the husband who took Israel as a wife (Isa. 54:5; Jer. 2:2). Ezekiel develops this further as God says to Israel, "Later I passed by, and when I looked at you and saw that you were old enough for love, I spread the corner of my garment over you and covered your nakedness. I gave you my solemn oath and entered into a covenant with you, declares the Sovereign LORD, and you became mine" (Ezek. 16:8). God chose to marry Israel.

In the opening story of this chapter, we saw Bill's delight in Sam's description of the outside world turn to bitterness, as jealousy so often does. A covenant quarrel also developed between God and Israel. God's "wife" chose the path of unfaithfulness. In the New Testament we come to the Book of James. James writes as though he has just been reading our most secret e-mail. He puts the issue of negative jealousy in the context of squabbles among Christians, particularly related to worldliness.

> What causes fights and quarrels among you? Don't they come from your desires that battle within you? You want something but don't get it. You kill and covet, but you cannot have what you want. You quarrel and fight. You do not have, because you do not ask God. When you ask, you do not receive, because you ask with wrong motives, that you may spend what you get on your pleasures.
>
> You adulterous people, don't you know that friendship with the world is hatred toward God? Anyone who chooses to be a friend of the world becomes an enemy of God. Or do you think Scripture says without reason that the spirit he caused to live in us envies intensely?
>
> James 4:1–5

These paragraphs have several references to sinful jealousy, using words like *covet, desires,* and *adulterous.* But we bypass the tempting issues of the passage to land on verse 5 where James refers to an Old Testament principle rather than a specific text. Did James intend to refer to our human spirits as the New International Version rendering indicates? Or might he have meant that the Holy Spirit is jealous for our attention to spiritual things? Perhaps James is contrasting human sinful jealousy with God's spiritual jealousy.

Prophet and Prostitute

Hosea is one of the most unusual books in the Bible. The prophet's name means "salvation," and he prophesied for nearly forty years between 760 and 722 B.C. Though the longest book of the Minor Prophets, it is referred to nowhere else in the Old Testament and only once in the New (Rom. 9:25). But the principles of this book appear nearly thirty times in the New Testament.

God actually said to this prophet, "Take to yourself an adulterous wife and children of unfaithfulness" (1:2). Most commentators believe Gomer's unfaithfulness occurred after the marriage and that this verse describes an attitude already ingrained in her at the time Hosea chose her. Gomer had three children but only one belonged to Hosea.

The purpose of Hosea's book (and of his bizarre behavior) emphasizes God's intent to show the heartache that he felt at the betrayal of his bride, Israel. The second chapter, however, describes Israel's future restoration with a new relationship, a new covenant, and a new blessing. Some sample verses will suffice for our brief study.

> "In that day," declares the LORD,
>   "you will call me 'my husband';
>   you will no longer call me 'my master.'

> I will betroth you to me forever;
>   I will betroth you in righteousness and justice,
>   in love and compassion.
> I will betroth you in faithfulness,
>   and you will acknowledge the LORD."

Hosea 2:16, 19–20

We see in Hosea this wonderful forgiving graciousness, this undeserved love, which he bestows on Gomer. Biblical jealousy, which is vigilant in guarding a possession, should make us want our wives and children for ourselves alone, but in the very best sense of that desire. Let's back up a bit.

In the Old Testament it seems clear that fathers were the heads of their families. One example appears in Nehemiah where we read, "On the second day of the month, the heads of all the families, along with the priests and the Levites, gathered around Ezra the scribe to give attention to the words of the Law" (Neh. 8:13). Dads learned the Bible in order to share their insights with their families. Their self-esteem rested not in being salesman of the month or senior vice president but in serving their families as priestly leaders. Biblical masculinity plays a significant role at every stage of a man's development. If we don't see ourselves as made-in-God's-image, we fail to bring biblical jealousy to the marriage partnership and can never quite grasp the parental role that follows the partner role.

Does the Bible lift one function above others for men, one task beyond everything else we do in our relationships with our wives and children? Without question it does. That responsibility is *loving* with the same sacrificial self-denial Christ demonstrated when he died for the world. Scripture applies the same Greek word to describe husband-love in Ephesians 5:25 and Colossians 3:19 as it does the love of the Savior in John 3:16.

Not only does a husband's love for his wife and children form the very foundation on which a marriage and family structure are built, it makes us like Hosea, willing to put up with everything from minor irritations to outright betrayal and still practice biblical jealousy as we father like the Father.

Practicing Biblical Jealousy

During his inaugural address at the opening of the Free University of Amsterdam in 1880, Abraham Kuyper, who later became prime minister of the Netherlands, challenged the audience with these words: "There is not one inch in the entire area of human life about which Christ, Who is sovereign of all, does not cry out, 'Mine!' "[2]

Our jealous God, who wants us to be vigilant in guarding the possession of family, which he has entrusted to us, has identified some areas in which he wants that positive jealousy demonstrated. There may be ten or fifteen such areas, but we think we can get the idea across by identifying just four.

Biblical Jealousy as Commitment

Only biblical people—people who have chosen to build relationships and determine their actions according to God's plan— can create Christian homes. You've already seen the orderly progression here—*biblical people become biblical partners who can then become biblical parents*. What do biblical fathers look like?

Is there some kind of special quality achieved or granted once and for all that turns us into people who somehow live on a higher plane? We could wish for some magic potion that could produce complete family commitment in our lives. In truth, however, becoming a biblical father is like everything else in life worth developing—it takes hard work and a series of increasingly complex commitments.

Fathering like the Father does not emerge from some rigid formula followed without deviation. This book centers on guiding principles drawn from Scripture (as well as years of fathering practice). Fathers who practice godly jealousy concerning their families usually demonstrate at least four commitments:

- a commitment to God's will
- a commitment to their wives
- a commitment to their children
- a commitment to lifelong love of family

None of these commitments can stand independently from the others. They start with God and end with love. Biblical fathers protect and develop loving relationships. In effective families, it is not the love that sustains the marriage but the marriage—the strong commitment—that sustains the love.

Biblical Jealousy as Covenant

All marriages include promises. Much of our family life rests on how well we keep them—not only between husband and wife but between parents and children. But this is not a society given to promise keeping. The enormous popularity of a men's group called Promise Keepers indicates something of the felt need for a higher sense of loyalty and stability, especially in the family.

This business of keeping covenants is close to God's heart. He once said to Noah, "Whenever I bring clouds over the earth and the rainbow appears in the clouds, I will remember my covenant between me and you and all living creatures of every kind" (Gen. 9:14–15). But by the time of Isaiah, the nation had taken on a more modern twist with respect to truth and trust: "The earth is defiled by its people; they have disobeyed the laws, violated the statutes and broken the everlasting covenant" (Isa. 24:5). Actually *commitment* and *covenant* sound very much like the same thing, but they are not. The *covenant* is the promise we make; the *commitment* is what we do about the promise. Biblical fathers should be promise keepers whether they attend the conventions or not. They make the covenant and keep the commitment.

Let's end this section with Eugene Peterson's paraphrase of Isaiah 54:10 in *The Message*. "For even if the mountains walk away and the hills fall to pieces, my love won't walk away from you, my covenant commitment of peace won't fall apart."

Biblical Jealousy as Relationship

We believe companionship stands as the primary purpose of marriage. In spite of all the wonderful things God created in the Garden of Eden, they were inadequate to meet Adam's need. None of the animals, splendid as they must have been before the fall, could provide a fitting companion for him. At that point the Lord created the first family. In Genesis 2:18 God said, "It is not good for the man to be alone. I will make a helper suitable for him." There it is again—*parenting follows partnering. Fathering depends on faithfulness.* The strategic role of the husband/wife relationship in marriage draws a bull's-eye on the family target. Everything else is secondary. Everything else takes a lower place of esteem, because when companionship doesn't work, the family can't function.

We fathers stand at the God-appointed pinnacle of our family units, so we're at the same time grateful, fearful, and hopeful regarding our task of leadership and our godly jealousy (covenant care) for our marriage relationships.

Biblical Jealousy as Lifestyle

What are we to make of Old Testament passages telling us that David and other godly men had multiple wives and yet God loved and blessed them? In looking at the flow of God's truth through both Testaments, we see the initial design as

God created it—one man and one woman in the Garden. Then sin entered the world, and all kinds of aberrations became common in human experience.

As much as we talk about committing ourselves to each other forever, we really mean until death. The fancy language in marriage ceremonies comes not only from years of church tradition but also from a solid biblical base. Yes, sometimes things go wrong and marriages end. In those agonizing experiences we turn to God's grace, not to judgmental harshness and finger-pointing. We are not perfect people, but that does not excuse us from working hard to live out our promises. Biblical jealousy involves a daily decision and desire to work on the marriage.

Let's remember that *fathering is not a formula* and *marriage is not mathematics*. As we develop our godly jealousy for our wives and children, God honors the committed covenant on which those relationships are based.

Jeff's Story

A slab of concrete tells my story in this chapter. A few weeks ago workers patched a section of our concrete driveway. It happened during the day while I worked, but my wife and children dutifully placed their handprints on the wet cement and etched their names into the slab. In the hope that I would return home in time to add my handprint, they scratched the word *Dad* alongside their names and hand impressions. Unfortunately, by the time I came home, the concrete had hardened. The word *Dad* is there, but without an accompanying handprint. Now each day when I walk up and down our driveway I am struck by a convicting, concrete illustration. I don't want to be a dad whose handprint is missing in the family! May I never appear *absent*, literally, emotionally, or spiritually. I must jealously guard the covenant I have with my family. Unless God takes me home to heaven, this dad will always be there.

Kenn's Story

The year was 1955 and I was a junior in college. In December I had dated a beautiful freshman girl and struggled in the second semester to make the relationship work. Numerous obstacles threatened my romantic goals, and I remember the names of most of them but won't recite them here. I experienced many emotions during those months—including acute jealousy. Every minute Betty spent with another boy, I agonized with internal feelings of envy, loss, and wounded pride. I experienced what Webster calls intolerance of rivalry, though no one else at that time seemed to appreciate the significance of my "ownership." It took the rest of that year to win my wife's hand; however, I made it past intolerance of rivalry to vigilance in guarding a possession. Feelings of jealousy, both negative and positive, seem to be a central part of romantic relationships. We experience them in ourselves, we help our children struggle through them, and we see them again in our grandchildren.

Making It Work

Chances are you have never heard a sermon on the jealousy of God, yet in this chapter we have only begun to explore the texts that emphasize this unique and easily misunderstood attribute. We consider jealousy a part of the aura in almost any family, a distinct component in the ambiance of human relationships. In addition to the part jealousy plays in romantic and marital relationships, it can envelop children as well. They can be jealous of each other and of the time and attention a parent spends on another child. Fathering like the Father requires not only an awareness of the role of jealousy in relationships but a battle plan to produce positive jealousy.

- Be willing to accept that jealousy has a positive side, even to the point of being grateful that your wife and children want more of you and your time.

- Examine your heart for any evidence of a need for positive jealousy. If family members have not been providing the kind of relationship you need, don't pout or become angry; talk to them directly about it and develop a strategy to improve in the future.
- Learn to practice a severe positive jealousy of your family above your job and career.

When you jealously guard your family relationships, you may turn down job offers that would require you to spend more time away from home, and you may even take a pay cut if the lower-salaried job allows you more time with your family. We've talked to lots of men who, at the end of their years, wish they had spent more time with their family. We have never met anyone who wishes he had spent more time at the office or on the job.

Crawford Loritts Jr. serves as an associate director with U.S. ministries under Campus Crusade for Christ and founded Legacy, an organization focused on helping to build strong, godly families in urban America. In an AMF (American Missionary Fellowship) newsletter interview, he urged dads to understand their mission.

> Your mission as a father is to present to the world a gift from your home to those who live on after you. The pressure of taking care of one crisis after another, and trying to make ends meet, easily distracts us from devoting time to this mission. It's unfair to our wives that so often we come home too tired from our jobs, our friends, and our social activities to have any joy or energy left for our children.[3]

These are timely words for properly jealous fathers on a mission. May God stoke the fires of our passion for building solid relationships with our children.

Questions for Discussion

1. How do you harmonize God's love and mercy with the attribute of jealousy?
2. Name some ways jealousy can help a family.

3. Review your covenant of marriage. Consider renewing it in some formal and public way. In fact think about how you might include your commitment to your children in that covenant.
4. What are the differences between positive and negative jealousy?

Father/Child Dialogue

1. Dad, describe for your kids the loving jealousy you have for your wife. Help them understand this positive attribute of God.
2. Kids, how would you describe your commitment to your family? Explain to your dad your understanding of positive jealousy.

six

Truth or Consequences

Attribute: Truthfulness
Text: Isaiah 45:19
Characters: Abraham and Isaac

> Truth is always strong, no matter how weak it looks, and falsehood is always weak, no matter how strong it looks.

> Phillips Brooks

We heard a story about a guy who showed his buddy the beautiful diamond ring he had bought his girlfriend for her birthday. The friend looked shocked and asked, "I thought she wanted a four-wheel-drive vehicle."

"That's right," he said, "but where am I going to find a fake jeep?"

When young women marry young men, they expect the real thing—not perfection but authenticity. And we don't mean the diamond or the car. Age is hardly an issue here and, unless they have been painfully disappointed too many times, most wives still expect the same thing fifty years later. Yet cheating on wives has almost become a cliché in America, a pattern of life literally modeled from coast to coast—in Washington and Hollywood.

Of course wives cheat on husbands too, but we wrote this book for men. Parents who cheat on each other also cheat on their children until the whole family loses its collective authenticity and becomes a sham. That's why the covenant of marriage, of which we speak so frequently in this book, is the very bedrock of family life.

But truth in fathering hardly limits itself to marital faithfulness. It encompasses the entire mind-set and lifestyle of how we behave in the family. In a helpful book, which could be considered a companion volume to this one, Michael Phillips talks about a period in his life when he struggled with a negative self-image and covered it up with moodiness. His bitterness turned into depression and even crept to the edges of paranoia. He writes,

> Other messages mingled with this internal imaging and produced a false image of my life. I believed that lie, and it left me with several decisions to make. And most of the ones I made were sinful. They resulted in more anguish, more pity, more depression, more suicidal thoughts and more bitterness.[1]

In this chapter we want to look at how truth as an attribute of God can permeate our lives as husbands and fathers. But first, as is our custom, we need a few glimpses at Scripture.

Friend and Fabricator

About four thousand years ago, a man by the name of Abram stepped out in faith, leaving his homeland and establishing his family in an entirely different area of the world. Surrounded by a strange culture and rampant paganism, he held on to one thing—his faith in God. One of the great verses of the Old Testament tells us, "Abram believed the LORD, and he credited it to him as righteousness" (Gen. 15:6). Yet this godly man, the father of a new nation, perhaps the leading candidate (with Moses and David) for the Old Testament MVP trophy, struggled to tell the truth.

This was no ordinary man. The Bible calls him a friend of God (Isa. 41:8; James 2:23). We learn from this great man that even godly people whose faith seems to radiate from their behavior are often tempted to tell less than the truth. We also learn the danger of such duplicity. When forced to enter Egypt because of famine, Abram feared what might happen to his beautiful wife, Sarah, so he instructed her in advance to tell the Egyptians she was his sister (a half-truth, since she was his half sister).

We might say he went to Egypt with God's permission rather than by the kind of direct call that brought him to Canaan in the first place. But the Bible never faults Abraham for making the trip; all human logic determined he had to find food. But it does catch him in the lie, as did the pharaoh of Egypt.

In this particular historical event, Abram's sin brought God's judgment on Pharaoh's house. In true demonstration of biblical grace, God overcame Abram's sin, forgave his lie, and sent him back to Canaan (Gen. 12:10–20).

I suspect Abram learned two important spiritual lessons from this side trip to Egypt—truth and trust. He exemplified the lesson of trust through the rest of his life on earth. The issue of truth, unfortunately, gave him difficulty again in chapter 20 where he told the same lie with essentially the same results!

Someone has argued that the best evidence for Christianity is Christians themselves—imperfect, sinful, broken people into whose lives God has brought forgiveness and restoration. Abram was like that—and so are we. Abram had to learn to pattern his life, including consistent truth-telling, after the very nature and character of God. We are so accustomed to lying as a cultural behavior that strict adherence to truth at times seems unusual, perhaps even impossible. But truth is built into the very fabric of God's being. God says of himself, "I, the LORD, speak the truth; I declare what is right" (Isa. 45:19). As John MacArthur says, "The only One we can trust without reservation is God. Because of His character, He cannot lie (Titus 1:2). Whatever He says or does is absolute truth. He has no ability to contradict Himself. When He makes a promise, He can't help but keep it. He never deviates from His will or His Word."[2]

As God's truth-nature reflects in us, we become real, authentic, genuine men whom people can trust. When we make promises to our children, we keep them. When we make covenants with our wives, we stand by them for life. A good leader does not surprise his followers; his consistency lets them know what to expect. Fathers are family leaders, and truthfulness and trustworthiness produce the kind of consistency that creates peace and stability in a family.

Our authenticity begins at home but carries over into our tasks at church. Many ask why men aren't stronger and more visible in twenty-first-century church leadership. We don't minimize the significant contribution of women throughout all the history of Christianity when we say the New Testament clearly emphasizes the leadership of truthful men in every congregation. Orthodox Judaism still follows the structure of a biblical synagogue requiring at least ten men for a service. In surrendering our economic responsibilities to the state and our religious responsibilities to professional clergy, we have stepped out of the role of authentic fatherhood and allowed surrogates to assume what God placed on our shoulders.

Families are hungry for truth in a society of falsehood—even if they don't know it. Your handling of Scripture at home is every bit as important as the way your pastor handles it at church. And your modeling of its principles in daily living is just as essential for your family as your pastor's behavior is for your congregation. There is no double standard. An old line says that truth is like a plant; it must first take root and then it bears fruit.

Along with many other Christian leaders, we fear that the relaxation of worship in our day may have already caused a de-emphasis on Bible exposition. God's truth—whether in the family or in the church—cannot be compressed into thirty-second sound bites, wall plaques, or little paperback books. When that happens our lives and our worship become self-focused rather than God-focused. And truth dissipates like a morning fog.

Combating the Culture

We live in a society whose people say whatever seems appropriate at the time. Philosophers call this behavior "existential," living for the moment and letting the future take care of itself. We watch this kind of mentality played out ad nauseam on television with politicians and celebrities. Say what is most convenient now, hope it works, and if not, simply contradict it later.

Postmodern people hardly think about what they say or even what they write. Neither of us watches television talk shows, but occasionally we stay up to watch Jay Leno do the headlines on

Monday night (why not—the football game lasts until midnight anyhow). But Jay is not the only one who collects headlines. The following examples come from David Grimes, a columnist for the *Herald-Tribune* in Sarasota, Florida.

British Study Finds Less Traffic When Roads Close
New Electric Car Would Run on Gasoline
Suicide Bomber Strikes Again
Retirement Will Be Cheaper If You Spend Less
Psychics Predict World Didn't End Yesterday
Queen Mary Having Bottom Scraped

And so it goes. Complete carelessness in speaking and writing mark our culture. In this kind of milieu, God needs men who will stand up and tell the truth—clearly, consistently, courageously—even when it may be harmful to them.

Erwin Lutzer, pastor of Moody Church, claims:

> Idolatry need not express itself in the construction of gold or silver statues. In fact, this activity is only the outward manifestation of the true spirit of idolatry, which is the process of creating God in our own image, and treating our opinions about God as the truth about God. Idolatry, harboring false thoughts about God, is attractive because it allows us to remain in control, at the center of our own world, defining our own standards and expectations.[3]

How does our culture pervert our thinking about God and truth? Certainly television is a prime source of truth decay. Author Douglas Groothuis warns, "As a visual medium it reduces the power of words, thereby creating an ethical and moral haze that insulates the young and impressionable—if not everyone else as well—from the truth." He recommends using "truth-enhancing" activities to counteract the corrosive effects of television on the minds and spirits of our children.[4]

In addition to television problems, our culture radiates a shabby understanding of and commitment to core values. Children kill other children at school. Employees blow up buildings because they feel they have been mistreated at work. Kids go to movies that pump hundreds of hours of violence and mayhem into their impressionable minds. For kids, the main thing now is to be *cool*. Being smart is okay, athletic is good too, and telling the truth may at times be useful, but whatever the cost, be *cool*. Some call the distributors of clothing, soft drinks, and other products that target children and teenagers the "merchants of cool" and claim they make billions of dollars by giving kids what they want.

And what do they want? First, an adult-free universe—which is why TV programs marketed to teens feature so few adults (or when adults do appear, they are portrayed as buffoons or hypocrites). Second, teens want to see, on television and movie screens, what New York University's Douglas Rushkoff calls a "version of themselves."

These versions are the template for two TV stereotypes: "mooks" and "midriffs." According to Chuck Colson, "mook is a character created to appeal to adolescent males, characterized by infantile, boorish behavior and trapped in a state of perpetual adolescence. Mooks are a staple on MTV. The midriff is, as Rushkoff describes her, a highly sexualized, world-weary sophisticate who manages to retain a bit of the little girl. Shows like *Boston Public* and singers like Britney Spears provide America's midriffs-in-training with role models to emulate."[5]

If television and marketing determine our kids' values and behavior, the battle for truth has ended and we have lost. This is not some stage your kids will outgrow. You're fighting for their minds and hearts, and if you are not prepared to lead the charge for truth by both living and teaching it, you have not just lost, you have surrendered.

Triumphing through Truth

Winning the battle for your family requires three things: truth-learning, truth-living, and truth-teaching. *Truth-learning* speaks for itself. Your careful and consistent involvement at church, your personal Bible study, your practice of spiritual disciplines such as prayer and meditation form the process of truth-learning in your life.

Truth-living means the authenticity and reality we've been talking about throughout this chapter. The old cliché says, "What you see is what you get." Your family should be able to see and experience truth through you.

We want to concentrate here on *truth-teaching*, which implies that you have truth-learning and truth-living reasonably well in hand. Genetic scientists have written extensively over the last five years regarding how people are shaped more by their genes than by their parents. Most is unconvincing and almost all of it unbiblical. At the very least, nurture is as important as nature, environment as important as heredity. In his book *The Relationship Code*, psychologist David Reiss of George Washington University claims, "Biology is not destiny. Many genetic factors, powerful as they may be in psychological development, exert their influence only through the good offices of the family."[6]

You may have heard about the second grader who brought home the report card that didn't meet his parents' expectations. After dinner Dad said, "Son, we are going to have to do something about these grades." To which the boy replied, "We can't, Dad. They're in ink." God's truth is like that—in ink. In a society of *relative* truth, we claim *absolute* truth grounded in Scripture, and that's what God expects us to teach.

We want to focus here on how you reflect God's truth in your family. Let's assume that you will emphasize truth in Bible teaching and family worship. But that assumption must be backed up by serious consequences for lying in your family discipline patterns. A four-year-old roaming loose around the house might very easily break an irreplaceable vase passed down from your great-grandmother. If your child comes in tears to ask forgiveness, you might have a word about not trying to clear the coffee table in one leap from the couch, but discipline is not called for (unless this has been a regular habit). On the other hand, if your child does not come to you, and an hour later you find the broken vase, and when you confront your child, she denies it, she has presented you with a dramatic truth-teaching moment. Even a child of four knows the difference between lies and truth, and breaking the vase becomes a minor incident compared to the lie.

And as we noted above, dads who teach God's Word to children must have adequate preparation. Picture the old Nike shoe commercial. Moses Malone (then with the Philadelphia 76ers) stands alone in an empty gymnasium throwing the ball up to the backboard and rebounding it—throwing it and rebounding it, throwing it and rebounding it—over and over. We hear no words until Moses finally turns toward the camera and says, "The way I figure it, before you shoot the ball you've got to get the ball." Dads who do not know God's Word and do not prepare for truth-teaching will find themselves inadequate and frustrated when trying to carry out their God-given commands and responsibilities.

Jeff's Story

I only meant to tap on the basement window with my foot. I knew my friends were hiding in the basement and I just wanted to give them a little scare. But my foot shattered the glass, and I took off running. When I got home (just a few doors away), I busied myself with some project, ignoring the mishap. But then my friends came to the door. I feigned shock and denied their accusations that I had broken the window. But as I closed the door, my eight-year-old body felt like it was melting under the weight of that sinful lie. With some truth-teaching help from my dad, I later confessed and paid for the window.

My children now love to hear that story and others like it because they represent "when dad did bad" times. But I don't mind telling these stories, because such lessons open the door for truth-teaching.

Kenn's Story

It was a wooden hanger and it hurt. I don't remember my age at the time, probably about eight or nine. My immigrant mother was a new Christian, and one of the rigid house rules required me to avoid the local movie theater—completely and without question. I can even remember the name of the flick—my first movie—*The Virginian*. Actually, I had a double problem; since I had sneaked into the theater, I had two reasons to lie about the event. Maybe that's why I got double whacks with the wooden hanger. I never used that particular punishment on my own children—nor do I recommend it to anyone else—but my mother's righteous indignation had been assaulted and she responded in a manner completely justified by her native Swiss culture. The fault was not hers; it was mine. I deserved the punishment and never entered that theater again.

Truth-teaching dads cannot allow lying to go unpunished in the family. But only truth-living dads can handle the problem with integrity.

Making It Work

Meanwhile, back in the Old Testament, God's friend Abraham (his name was changed by the time Isaac was born) reproduces his worst behavior in his own son! Like Yogi Berra, we find déjà vu all over again. In Genesis 26 we read, "When the men of that place asked him about his wife, he said, 'She is my sister,' because he was afraid to say, 'She is my wife.' He thought, 'The men of this place might kill me on account of Rebekah, because she is beautiful' " (v. 7). When we model half-truths or outright lies, we can expect that our children will acquire the same dubious skill. How can we tell the truth and teach the truth to our kids? Consider these suggestions:

- Make a commitment to always tell the truth to your wife and your children. Voice that commitment to them.
- In your family discipline patterns, lay down some serious consequences for lying. Make a clear distinction between childish mistakes and intentional lies.
- Communicate with your kids so that you can contradict errors your children may collect in the general business of living—the science teacher at school who mocks the idea of creation; a friend who brags about how much he gets away with because his parents don't know; the temptation to cheat on a test to keep up with the academic pressures at school. These are *teachable moments* for godly parents who want to become triumphant truth-teachers.

- Don't get discouraged. Every parent fails with discouraging regularity. Urban Hilger, president of the Dalmo-Victor division of the Singer Company, tells about his first day on the ski slopes. He skied all day long and didn't fall once, so he proudly announced that achievement to his instructor at the end of the day. The instructor's response shocked Hilger: "Personally, Urban, I think you had a lousy day. If you're not falling, you're not learning."

Reflect on your most profound learning experiences. Were they when you eased through a new task without any significant error or were they when you had to redo and experiment and keep coming back to finish the task properly? Of course we want our children to learn our spiritual heritage, but we all fail, and in those times we remember the never-tiring grace of God.

Failure may mean disappointment, but it does not mean defeat. In fact experimentation is probably essential for truth-teaching. Sometimes you may feel like that novice lion tamer being interviewed by a reporter on a slow news day:

"I understand your father was also a lion tamer."

"Yes, he was."

"Do you actually put your head into the lion's mouth?"

"I did it only once—to look for Dad."

God will not allow Christians to shift family accountability to churches or schools or other organizations. Teachers are important, but in the role of nurture they are bench players—substitutes for parents. Through all the years of parental relationships, God expects truth-teaching to be one of our major responsibilities.

Questions for Discussion

1. Think about a "wooden hanger" incident in your life. How did your parents teach you that lying is unacceptable?
2. What issues are active in your children's lives right now that could impinge on their ability to reflect God's character of truth? How can you help them resolve those issues?

3. Talk about some ways you can improve on your truth-learning. Could you do more serious Bible study, take notes during the pastor's sermon, read about the truth distortion in contemporary culture?

Father/Child Dialogue

1. Dad, during some peaceful family time when no discipline or punishment issues appear on the agenda, talk to your children about truth and how important it is to God and to you.

2. Kids, think about any dishonesty that may be going on in your life right now, not necessarily a lie that you've told but perhaps something hidden from your parents that you know they really should hear about. Sometimes we call this "lying by just keeping quiet."

seven

God's Friend

Divine Attribute: Friendship
Text: James 2:23
Character: Abraham

So long as we love we serve. No man is useless while he is a friend.

Robert Louis Stevenson

Every year on Father's Day children send more than one hundred million cards to their dads. According to the Hallmark people, nearly one in four carries a humorous message, compared with one in seven humorous Mother's Day cards. Try the following contrast as an example:

You're such a great Dad. You deserve a 21-gun salute—would you settle for 10 belches, 7 knuckles cracking, and 4 armpit sounds?

You can count on a mother's love . . . like the sun rising each day . . . and May flowers blooming every year.

Not only do we get lampooned more than Mom, sometimes even Mother's Day cards take a shot at us.

It's Mother's Day, Mom, and I just wanted to say—thanks for stomping that imaginary brake that way when Dad drives. Probably saved our lives dozens of times.

If greeting cards give any clue, Americans still put mothers on a pedestal, with dads standing around watching. Americans have always believed that a father should be a tower of strength and, as such, probably doesn't need much encouragement. We ought to be able to roll with any punches, even sarcastic humor on a card. Father's Day cards commonly omit words like "sweet, sensitive, tender," which card makers reserve for Mom and Mother's Day.

Those macho-dad images can mask the softer side of fathering. We want to emphasize that fathering like the Father means becoming friends to our children without surrendering the family headship role. Secretary of State Colin Powell talks about his father:

> Remembering him fondly on Father's Day, I realize how much of my own success I owe to his example. And when I think of that, I worry about the great many young people who will not be spending today with their own fathers. Nearly 40 percent of our children are growing up without a father at home. Some sociologists predict that this figure could reach 50 percent in the next few years. It is a cruel and life-warping deprivation.[1]

Our primary character for this chapter will be Abraham and our launchpad text, James 2:23: "And the scripture was fulfilled that says, 'Abraham believed God, and it was credited to him as righteousness, and he was called God's friend.'" Abraham obeyed God even to the point of offering his son Isaac on the altar. Because of Abraham's obedience, God initiated a close relationship with him and called the first patriarch, "God's friend." What forms does friendship take as we look up to our fathers and down to our children? How can we spin off God's relationship with Abraham to become father-friends at home?

Friendship as Attitude

Josh McDowell talks about the violence and fierce brutality of today's young people who feel lost and disconnected. He claims that their pain and antisocial behavior arise from a sense of alienation and aloneness that can only be effectively combated by strong relational connections with their parents. Josh offers parents a simple formula.

Rules minus Relationship = Rebellion
Rules plus Relationship = Positive Response[2]

Young lives that used to revolve around family, church, school, and friends now live in cyberspace chat rooms and "stay in touch" through e-mail and cell phones. Experts claim that more than 70 percent of teenagers will be Internet connected by the year 2003. Single parents head one in four U.S. families. The TV families of the twenty-first century would have us believe that two-thirds of all families are run by a single mom or dad. And when the TV dad is on his own, watch out—it's chaos city. Television fathers are funny, stupid, crude, vulgar, and selfish—but few of them model genuine friendship.

The New Testament uses the word *friend* in both a personal and social sense. In the personal sense it takes the same meaning we would use today, a trusted and valued companion. In the social sense it simply describes political relationships as in Mark Anthony's famous speech, "Friends, Romans, Countrymen." In John 19:12, the crowds scream at Pilate, threatening him with the warning, "If you let this man go, you are no friend of Caesar." Why did they choose that piercing argument, probably the very words that ultimately led Pilate to decide Jesus' fate? Because in the Roman world friendship implied an intimate, trusting relationship.

To be "a friend of Caesar" meant four things. First, it meant that the person knew the emperor intimately. "Friends of Caesar" would actually open the emperor's mail and carry on his correspondence. They knew him that well. Second, it meant that the friend was willing to go wherever the emperor sent him. "Friends of Caesar" would often be sent to the provinces to do business for the emperor. There they would represent him and conduct his affairs. Third, "a friend of Caesar" retained the title even if the emperor died. "A friend of Caesar" remained a friend of the Roman Empire. Fourth, if the friend betrayed the emperor, he would lose his privileged status and this would mean his political doom.[3]

The foundational attitude for friendship is trust—Abraham trusted God, and God trusted Abraham. Friends usually *do* lots of things for us, but what makes them friends is the way they *think* about us. Attitude means more than action. We live this out in a number of ways, but one simple earthly illustration is the tennis court. We both play tennis and we prefer to play together rather than against each other. For one thing, we both know each other's strengths and weaknesses, and in a competitive game like tennis, we feel compelled to exploit those weaknesses to help our doubles partners. When we play together, we frequently win. Over the past five years we have probably played fifty or sixty matches as partners and have won more than 90 percent of them. Sounds a bit like bragging, but neither of us is, by himself, a great tennis player. Kenn rarely plays singles, and Jeff, for all his speed and youthful energy, loses probably twice as many singles matches as doubles.

What makes the difference? It's not speed, wisdom, or athletic ability. It's that we know each other and trust each other on the court. We have deliberately designed our doubles strategy to complement one another and we play as a team. We don't criticize, complain, argue, or whine. We expect that each will do his best on any given day, and that's all we can ask, whatever the outcome.

In the same way, your friendship with your children depends on your attitude toward them and their attitude toward you. Hostility, fear, anger, and moodiness tear down genuine friendship, whether displayed by parents or children. Remember, when we look at our biblical model, we say that God exemplifies the father's role and Abraham the child's. God initiated the relationship. *Initiating* friendship with his children and acting on it are a father's responsibility.

Friendship as Presence

An old *Reader's Digest* story tells about a man who testified at the trial of an organized-crime boss and then begged to be put into the witness-protection program. The FBI responded by getting him a job as a salesclerk at Kmart. After five years no one's been able to find him!

With apologies to Kmart (only halfhearted), let's recognize that in too many families nobody can find Dad, and not just because he bailed out and ditched the family, though that happens more frequently than we like to think. The sad reality is that many fathers who work hard to support their families and really love their families, injure them repeatedly by not being available when needed. Abraham is the only person in the Bible called "a friend of God." That phrase appears not only in the James passage cited above, but in 2 Chronicles 27:7 and Isaiah 41:8. The Isaac-on-the-altar story dramatically illustrates how God manifested himself whenever Abraham needed him.

Abraham could be God's friend because they knew each other intimately. Theologians use both *immanence* and *transcendence* to describe God. The latter word emphasizes how God differs from us, so much higher and greater and distant. *Immanence*, on the other hand, focuses on God our Father and God our Friend. This is the image we as dads need to emulate. Leaders at parenting conferences often say things like, "Your kids need more of you and less of your money," which is exactly true. Part of the commitment we talked about in chapter 5 focuses right here on the issue of presence at home.

Presence is a hot theme in today's parenting literature and not just in evangelical circles. In the October 30, 2000, issue of *U.S. News & World Report*, Katy Kelly writes:

> In order to raise emotionally healthy and protected children, the doctors stated in an interview that kids' number one need is a nurturing, consistent connectedness with a parent or other important adult. This goal can be achieved only when society begins to put children first and revolve everything else around them—including our jobs.[4]

Kelly quotes famous pediatricians Barry Brazelton and Stanley Greenspan, whose book *The Irreducible Needs of Children* emphasizes how parents need to spend more significant childcaring time at home, probably until their children reach their middle to late teens.

The payoff comes at the other end. We both consider ourselves each other's best friend, even though we've had dozens of contacts with other friends down through the years. In addition to those hours on the tennis court, we go to lunch about once a week (when our schedules coincide) and stay in touch by phone or e-mail when geographically separated. At sixty-seven Kenn thinks it's important for Jeff to understand that his devotion to his son has not waned just because that son is now a middle-aged adult responsible for his own family. Jeff, on the other hand, remembering those many years of hiking, biking, swimming, and playing basketball together, still makes every effort to involve his dad in as many activities as possible. Attitude means how we think about friendship between ourselves and our children; presence means being there in the flesh.

Friendship as Togetherness

In his 1999 book *Becoming Dad*, syndicated columnist Leonard Pitts Jr. *(Miami Herald)* describes his struggle to become a quality father despite having grown up with an alcoholic and abusive dad.[5] He subtitles his book *Black Men and the Journey to Fatherhood*. Certainly, fatherless children come in every color, but Pitts became particularly disturbed after seeing U.S. census figures showing 64 percent of black children are raised in single-parent households. In his research Pitts talked with hundreds of black men who, to his surprise, seemed quite willing to talk about this vacuous area of their lives. Like families without fathers, fathers without families are incomplete, regardless of the reason for the separation. So friendship is not only *attitude* and *presence*, it is *togetherness*—father and child doing things together. Without attitude and presence, however, there can be no togetherness.

Christian families ought to be like teams with Dad serving as coach. He may not be the star player, and he may not call all the plays, but he's responsible for the success or failure of the team. Both of us are avid basketball fans and annually put a dinner on the line by predicting the outcomes of all the games in the NCAA tournament. We won't say who wins most frequently (lest Jeff be embarrassed), but one team we both like year after year is the Duke Blue Devils. In 1991 Duke upset UNLV in the semifinal game of the tournament. According to Coach Mike Krzyzewski, the basketball system at Duke emphasizes communication and honesty on and off the court, role acceptance, leadership responsibilities, and maximum effort. Coach K claims, "As soon as the team realizes it has the group mentality, it can assume a group identity, and any combination of five players can play as one."[6] What a great definition of a team and a great definition of a family—a group of people with a common identity and group mentality! Leadership in family togetherness is ministry, just as much ministry as serving as an elder, deacon, pastor, or missionary. Men must recognize this biblical priority. God's description of the kind of man he wants in congregational leadership emphasizes faithfulness in family life (1 Tim. 3:4–5, 11–13). The New Testament word for *ministry* or *service* is *diakonia*. Jesus used it of himself in saying to his disciples, "I am among you as one who serves" (Luke 22:27). We do the New Testament and the Lord of the church a great disservice by reserving that common and gentle word for clergy and missionaries. As dads, we serve the Lord when we serve our families. But Jesus also called that serving relationship a friendship. He said to his disciples, "I no longer call you servants, because a servant does not know his master's business. Instead, I have called you friends, for everything that I learned from my Father I have made known to you" (John 15:15). As a servant leader to his disciples, Jesus taught them everything they knew about ministry and, in so doing, built an intimate relationship with them that he called "friendship." Mark describes Jesus' mentoring philosophy with these simple words, "He appointed twelve—designating them apostles—that they might be with him and that he might send them out to preach and to have authority to drive out demons" (Mark 3:14–15). Togetherness in ministry produced friendship and leadership.

As servant-leader dads to our children, we coach them and teach them based on what we have learned from our heavenly Father. And that time spent together translates into friendship. Just as we must take time to develop our friendship/relationship with Christ, we do the same with our children. As Carl Laney puts it, "To be a friend of Christ means more than simply knowing certain facts about him. You can know God's attributes and not know him personally. But to be a friend of Christ means that

you have a growing, vital, dynamic relationship which is culti-
vated by the study of God's Word and prayer."[7]

As father and son, we teach doctoral seminars together,
preach at Bible conferences together, sing duets together, vacation together with our families, sit together at social events on
the campus where we both live, and more or less live our lives
side by side.

For some fathers and children, geographical realities preclude
this kind of togetherness. Sometimes personalities of other family members get in the way or perhaps inadequate finances keep
us from being as close to our children as we would like. But we
have written this book to tell you it is worth the effort to take
togetherness between fathers and children to the highest possible level and maintain it carefully, keeping it emotionally, spiritually, and socially tuned like a new Mercedes.

Friendship as Love

On any given night in the United States, one hundred thousand homeless children live on our streets. Children under eighteen are the fastest-growing age group among the homeless, a
scandal of outrageous proportions. Not only do many of these
children have no homes, they also have no parents. Physically
absent and irresponsible fathers account for the major portion
of childhood poverty.

Today about one-third of American children—twenty-one million—live away from their fathers. Among the children of divorce,
half have never even visited their fathers' homes. In a typical year,
40 percent of them don't see their fathers at all. One-fifth of the
children of divorce have not seen their fathers in five years.[8]

Years ago Alvin Toffler warned us in *Future Shock* that par-
enthood remains the greatest single preserve of the amateur.
Divorce, drug abuse, alcoholism, child abuse, spouse abuse, and
hundreds of other family failures unfurl a black curtain across
the stage of modern American life. Against that backdrop God
calls many Christian men in our culture to engage in the biblical activity of *fathering*. If we approach it as a biblical activity,
we grow in our understanding of what God expects of us to
whom he gives this important responsibility.

The Bible says a great deal more about husbands loving their wives than their children, perhaps on the assumption that if they achieve the first, the second will follow. Indeed, the one biblical command most heavily emphasized for married men tells them to love their wives. Have a look at a few verses from Ephesians 5:

> And you husbands, show the same kind of love to your wives as Christ showed to the church when he died for her. . . . That is how husbands should treat their wives, loving them as parts of themselves. For since a man and his wife are now one, a man is really doing himself a favor and loving himself when he loves his wife! . . . a man must love his wife as a part of himself.
>
> Ephesians 5:25, 28, 33 TLB

The Greek word for love *(agape)* appears in all the marriage and family sections of the New Testament. This word speaks of the kind of love only produced in the heart of a person by the presence of the Holy Spirit. It appears as the fruit of the Spirit in Galatians 5:22, the love of God for the world in John 3:16, the love of Christ for humanity in 1 John 2:16–17, and the love of a husband for his wife in Ephesians 5:25–33 and Colossians 3:19. Throughout the chapters in Genesis that tell his story, we learn very clearly how much Abraham loved Sarah and Isaac as well. His love for Ishmael functioned at a lower level, and one could argue that the front pages of our newspapers today describing the Israeli/Arab war in Palestine merely remind us of conflicts that began in Abraham's tent so many centuries ago. Love for and friendship with our wives sets the model of love for and friendship with our children.

Earlier we mentioned that we occasionally speak together at conferences and also on occasion introduce each other on the platforms of some of these venues. We have found these times to be some of the most foolish and funny moments of our lives together. As we "dig" each other with jokes from the pulpit, we are showing love and indicating that our relationship is strong enough to heckle each other in public and laugh together at the results. The kind of father/child friendship we describe in this chapter does not tiptoe around each other's fragile pride or nervous emotions. It is open, complete, vulnerable, totally masculine, and healthy.

An old story tells about a man who walked down the street and fell in a hole too deep to climb out. A doctor walked by, asked if he noticed any major injuries from the fall and, hearing of none, continued on his way. A priest came by, sprinkled some holy water down the hole, and wished God's blessing on the fallen man. A few minutes later a good friend came by and without a moment's hesitation jumped down into the hole with him. The man in the hole looked at this friend and said, "Are you crazy? Isn't it bad enough that I fell down here and can't get out? Why in the world would you jump in with me?" "Relax," said the friend, "I've been in this hole before and I know the way out."

Being a father-friend may mean jumping into holes on more than one occasion, holes you've seen before, holes whose dangers and fears you know, but holes out from which you've successfully climbed in the past and now can help your children do the same. Since God is our model throughout this book, let's note that he fell into a hole too, in the person of his Son Jesus Christ. The writer of Hebrews says, "Since the children have flesh and blood, he too shared in their humanity so that by his death he might destroy him who holds the power of death—that is, the devil—and free those who all their lives were held in slavery by their fear of death" (Heb. 2:14–15).

Becoming a friend like the Father is not easy. We started with some interesting contrasts between Father's Day and Mother's Day; let's pursue a similar observation. When a television camera zooms in on an athlete who has just made a great play, he says, "Hi, Mom," not, "Thanks, Dad." But probably Dad taught him how to make that catch. When well-behaved children leave the table after a good meal, they may express appreciation to Mom for her hard work in cooking it, but rarely if ever appreciation for Dad whose hard work bought the food and the cooking utensils. At Christmas the kids open presents with delight and thank Mom, since they assume she did the shopping and the wrapping. They forget that Dad's ten-hour days at the office bought the present and the paper. It's the Rodney Dangerfield syndrome, and we just learn to live with it. The eloquence of Paul Harvey puts it better than we can.

A father is a thing that is forced to endure childbirth without an anesthetic. . . . A father never feels worthy of the worship in a child's eyes. He's never quite the hero his daughter thinks, never quite the man his son believes him to be and this worries him, sometimes. So he works too hard to try and smooth the rough places in the road for those of his own who will follow him. . . . Fathers are what give daughters away to other men who aren't nearly good enough, so they can have grandchildren who are smarter than anybody's. Fathers make bets with insurance companies about who will live the longest. One day they lose and the bet's paid off to the part of them they leave behind.[9]

Jeff's Story

Nearly every sport and game I play, I learned from my dad. We have always been and will always be each other's best male friend. Over the last twelve years we have added another Gangel male into our fraternity, my son, Brad. Now I pass on to my son what I learned from my dad. Occasionally we spend time together as three best friends, playing golf, eating pizza, watching football, stacking wood, or even pestering Grandma! I firmly believe that God intends us to befriend our children. I benefited from that relationship, and now my son benefits too.

Kenn's Story

I admit from the outset that Jeff has the upper hand on this chapter. My father was never my friend; I hardly knew him at all. So I can only look down at the great relationship Jeff and I have had for more than forty years, one of the great treasures of my life. But he can look both up and down the ladder of chronology, experiencing those forty years with me and another twelve with young Bradley. My son is without question my closest friend (apart from my wife).

As an only child whose parents divorced when I was ten, I remember no Christmases at home after my tenth birthday. My wife, Betty, on the other hand, is still closely tied to her two sisters and her brother and, until Betty went off to college, the whole family had lived for decades within a few miles of each other in southwestern Ohio.

As she and I talked about this wider family togetherness even before our wedding, we determined to make an effort to keep our children in touch with their aunts, uncles, and cousins as much as possible. That led to designing an annual trip to Dayton, Ohio, from wherever we lived at the time. Sometimes we braved horrible ice storms to make the trip; other times it took two days each way with all the expense such a journey incurs. But we achieved our goals.

Jeff and his sister are still in close touch with almost all their cousins and frequently visit them when they're in the area of southwestern Ohio. We achieved this by spending between one and two weeks at Betty's home every Christmas for thirty years (an experience that often pushed togetherness beyond our comfort zones).

Making It Work

One day when Jeff was just about five years old, Kenn went into the parents' bedroom and saw him sitting on the edge of the bed looking in the mirror with a somewhat pensive look on his face. The conversation sounded something like this.

"Son, what are you doing?"

"Looking in the mirror."

"I can see that, but why are you sitting on our bed looking in the mirror in the middle of the day?"

"Dad, people tell me I look like you. Do I really look like you?"

"Yes, son, you do, and I apologize about that, but you're just going to have to learn to live with it."

"Dad, I'm going to go wherever you go and I'm going to do whatever you do so maybe when I'm big like you I'll look even more like you than I do now."

For Kenn, that lesson was worth three weeks of Bible conference on parenting. Fathers are the mandatory models for their children. You don't have a choice.

But what do dads model? More to the point, what can we do to create the friendship setting our children so desperately need?

- Demonstrate obedience to God in every aspect of the family context, and serve Christ in a way that reflects friendship with him.
- Be there for your children when they need you the most. Make it a priority!
- Reflect God's kindness, forgiveness, discipline, and love so that your children can see the heavenly Father in you and learn to trust him as their friend too.
- Look for ways, even at the earliest ages, to spend time with your children; do things you both enjoy and form a close bond.

Modeling and *mentoring* are buzzwords today. Men's groups, such as Promise Keepers and Point Men, challenge men by the thousands to face their responsibilities in family, church, and world, to put aside small-mindedness, materialism, and self-centeredness, and get on with the task of being godly men. We applaud such emphasis and the great good that comes from these organizations. But let's not let all that enthusiastic encouragement make us feel inadequate. We can find great joy and value in friendship with our children when they are young, and those rewards only appreciate as they become independent adults.

Questions for Discussion

1. Why do you think God initiated a friendship with Abraham? Why did Jesus initiate a friendship with his disciples?
2. In your opinion, why are there not more Bible characters called friends of God?
3. Of the four characteristics of friendship presented in this chapter (attitude, presence, togetherness, love), which one needs your greatest attention?

4. Does your relationship (friendship) with your children need to be repaired in any way or tuned up just a bit? What can you do about it?

Father/Child Dialogue

1. Dad, tell your kids about a great friend you had when you were their ages (perhaps their grandfather). Talk about things you did together and how those memories continue.
2. Kids, tell Dad about your best friends at school or in the neighborhood. Why did you choose them? Then talk about what you most love doing with your dad.

eight

The Child Whisperer

Attribute: Communication
Texts: Deuteronomy 6:1–2; John 1:1, 14
Character: Asaph

We can communicate an idea around the world in seventy seconds, but it sometimes takes years for an idea to get through one-fourth inch of human skull.

Charles Kettering

The simplest and best definition of communication we have ever seen consists of just two words—*meaning exchange*. Communication is not word exchange (people hurling verbs and nouns at each other) but meaning exchange. The communication process is dynamic and always in operation when people confront each other. These dynamics come into play in every human relationship, yet we spend so little time thinking about the process. Many of the problems we face in Christian families today result in a breakdown of communication. People do not always say what they mean, as any sports fan knows.

- "We have only one person to blame, and that's each other" (Barry Beck, New York Ranger, on who started a brawl during the National Hockey League's Stanley Cup play-offs).

- "The doctors x-rayed my head and found nothing" (Dizzy Dean, explaining how he felt after being hit on the head by a ball in the 1934 World Series).
- "It could permanently hurt a batter for a long time" (Pete Rose, complaining about a brushback pitch).
- "Me and George and Billy are two of a kind" (Mickey Rivers, on his warm relationship with George Steinbrenner and Billy Martin).
- "I have never had major knee surgery on any other part of my body" (Winston Bennett, University of Kentucky basketball forward).
- "Winfield goes back to the wall! He hits his head on the wall and it rolls off! It's rolling all the way back to second base! This is a terrible thing for the Padres!" (Jerry Coleman, Padres' announcer, telling fans about a fly ball).
- "The similarities between me and my father are different" (Dale Berra, Yogi's son).

Some of those are rather scary—especially that last one, which suggests a genetic propensity toward communication problems. We can be thankful that God has chosen to communicate clearly with his children. God gave his decrees to Israel (Deut. 6:1–2) and spoke his Word to the world (John 1:1, 14). And God speaks to us in Scripture (2 Peter 1:19–21). God says what he means and means what he says. If we as fathers want to do the same, we need three things—purpose, content, and results.

Communicate with Purpose

One of the great New Testament passages on modeling starts off talking about mothers and ends up talking about fathers (1 Thess. 2:6–12). Here's the text of verses 10–12:

> You are witnesses, and so is God, of how holy, righteous and blameless we were among you who believe. For you know that we dealt with each of you as a father deals with his own children, encouraging, comforting, and urging you to live lives worthy of God, who calls you into his kingdom and glory.

Obviously, communication contains many more purposes than encouragement, comfort, and exhortation, but the point is that these three must be included. In the Thessalonians passage the idea of encouragement and comfort gives us a glimpse at two themes Paul deals with frequently in his writing. He often uses the word *encouragement* to describe God's ministry to us, but *comfort* is always a human word, never used directly to mean God's comfort. It describes the way God works through people to minister to others—like the way he uses fathers to minister to children. The word *exhortation* carries the idea of urgency— admonishing or witnessing truth so that our children walk in patterns acceptable to God. These words imply a peaceful family where order rather than chaos marks each day. God wants to give dads peace and he wants them to instill that peace into the lives of their children whose culture already knows too much trouble and turmoil.

How can we communicate encouragement, comfort, and truth to our children? One way is to *make sure we do not portray a distant and angry God*. Small children especially see in their parents a picture of God. If life seems constantly negative and punitive, they reason, God must be like that. A child's relationship with his or her father shapes the child's earliest ideas about God.

Second, we reflect the heavenly Father by *making sure we do not squelch the unfailing love he wants to show others through us*. We draw on God's grace for our own needs and that's very important, but we must also be channels of that grace to our children.

Third, *never let present struggles detract from future blessings*. Parents can easily get entangled with some current crisis and lose sight of long-range goals.

In Paul Randolph's fine research on family covenants, he talks about understanding a child's view of God and describes one counselee who saw God as capricious, angry, and quick to punish.

It came partly from some legalistic teaching in her church. But a major source of this misunderstanding was the way she transferred her concept of her earthly father to her heavenly Father. Her father was very legalistic with his children. There was a rule for everything. When I talked to the father about this, he felt he was simply following God's example. God to him was the ultimate rule-maker and enforcer—a cosmic Moses and Dirty Harry all rolled into one!

How a family communicates its understanding of God can tell you a lot about their problems and the underlying heart issues. I normally ask children and their parents a lot of questions about their understanding of God. I not only want to know what kind of devotional life they have but what kind of God they worship and what role He has in their lives.[1]

Communicate Important Content

An interesting passage lies tucked away at the beginning of Psalm 78:

> O my people, hear my teaching;
>   listen to the words of my mouth.
> I will open my mouth in parables,
>   I will utter hidden things, things from of old—
> what we have heard and known,
>   what our fathers have told us.

Psalm 78:1–3

These words come from Asaph, a member of a family of singers who assisted in temple worship. Notice how many words in these few verses emphasize what fathers teach. Too many parents today show a tendency to worship at academic altars. We want our children to have the best education and urge them to do well in school all the time. We see education as the way to obtain economic power and too often we place it ahead of character development and a healthy spiritual life. Others take the opposite extreme, fearing that the development of an active intellectual life will lead to a denial of basic truth. Both probably reflect error. Our friend Asaph avoids confusion by centering his emphasis on content—something specific must be taught.

This entire psalm focuses on the centrality of the Bible. Today we have much more of the Bible than Asaph had, and godly fathers still hold Scripture central to all they teach. Remember, Christian teaching finds its primary role in spiritual maturation not the accumulation of information. We do not deny the importance of the works of Plato, Beethoven, and Einstein, but they do not represent the central focus for Christian teaching. God reserves that place for his Word.

In Christian families, authority wraps itself in the content handed down from grandparents to parents to children. Of course not every family functions that way, since not all grandparents and parents are believers. But this displays God's ideal. In these verses we have a reminder to protect the spiritual heritage of our families by making sure that we take our teaching responsibilities seriously.

Jesus once warned religious teachers of his day by saying, "Woe to you experts in the law, because you have taken away the key to knowledge. You yourselves have not entered, and you have hindered those who were entering" (Luke 11:52). As dads, we must ask if we open the doors to spiritual content or keep them tightly shut by making the Bible confusing, boring, or unapproachable. This mysterious verse in Luke ought to haunt the days and nights of every father. These men Jesus rebuked should have provided the key to understanding Scripture, but they had not entered into the meaning themselves and therefore withheld motivation and comprehension from other people.

We communicate clear content to achieve specific purposes. As our psalm continues, Asaph reminds dads:

> We will not hide them from their children;
>   we will tell the next generation
> the praiseworthy deeds of the LORD,
>   his power, and the wonders he has done.
> He decreed statutes for Jacob
>   and established the law in Israel,
> which he commanded our forefathers
>   to teach their children.
> so the next generation would know them,
>   even the children yet to be born,
>   and they in turn would tell their children.
> Then they would put their trust in God
>   and would not forget his deeds
>   but would keep his commands.

Psalm 78:4–7

When parents communicate, their children don't have to guess what they hold true and valuable. Today, however, many parents don't try to communicate but allow their children to make their own ethical and moral choices. Almost all public education urges children to select the best among alternatives, not to embrace the absolute morality of the Bible. But God wills the communication of his truth to children in the family. Do we communicate to our children that God is unloving, uncaring, and capricious or that God has a history of redemptive activity toward those he loves and to whom he has committed himself? By understanding and communicating the long-term history of God's actions, we may help our children know the framework for the belief that will carry them through the present difficult times.

Communicate for Results

The staggering conclusion of our passage in Psalm 78 finds Asaph asking for children who are better than their fathers:

> They would not be like their forefathers—
> a stubborn and rebellious generation,
> whose hearts were not loyal to God
> whose spirits were not faithful to him.

Psalm 78:8

So families *do* go bad and the chain of teaching God's truth does not always stand unbroken. Notice that all these sins reflect behaviors quite common in our society today. Christian dads must work to produce biblical qualities, which, like all Christian standards, tend to be countercultural. Asaph bemoans the recollection that these forefathers were stubborn, rebellious, disloyal, and faithless. God's children must be flexible, obedient, loyal, and faithful.

Since both of us have experienced parenting teenagers, we like to say that parents get the teenagers they create. Yes, young adults may turn away from the teaching of their parents and wander down different paths, but teenagers are the direct result of twelve years of parenting. We have no more right to complain about their behavior than about what we find on our plates at the end of a buffet line.

Nevertheless, we don't always get the results we want any more than we get the answers we want when we ask children questions. Trudy Zmerold tells about her three-year-old daughter, Katie, who was taken to her pediatrician during a recent bout with the flu. As the doctor examined her ears, he asked, "Will I find Big Bird in here?" Apprehensively, Katie answered, "No." Then, before examining her throat, he asked, "Will I find the Cookie Monster in here?" Again, "No." Finally, listening to her heart he asked, "Will I find Barney?" With innocent conviction, she looked him directly in the eye and said, "No, Jesus is in my heart. Barney is on my underwear!"[2]

Communication is meaning exchange. Say what you mean and mean what you say.

Jeff's Story

While we must try to connect the lines of communication at all times, we know that kids log on better at certain times. Often the busy work schedules that keep dads hopping limit our time with our children. This is all the more reason we must capitalize on the special times.

For my kids and me, bedtime has become our communication time. I intentionally crawl onto the bed and tussle until the words spill out. I hear questions and comments that never squirm out of their bodies during the busy day. I also plan occasional outings when I spend time with just one child. A few weeks ago I took my daughter to see *Annie*. We had to drive more than an hour each way to get there, but what a great communication commute! We talked about subjects we'd never discussed before. If you want to communicate more with your children, you must plan for it.

Kenn's Story

A temperamental loner at heart, I have had to learn to communicate effectively on an interpersonal level. For me, speaking from a platform (preaching, lecturing, or teaching) is a piece of cake compared to one-on-one conversation. A doctoral minor in organizational communications helped me learn that I am essentially a very private person who prefers to achieve with deeds rather than talk. I have always liked the tongue-in-cheek line, "After all is said and done, more is said than done."

So I still have to make careful effort to listen to other people, to try to understand the emotional context from which they speak, and to frame my answers in ways that will not be offensive and yet will clearly say what I mean. When it comes to warm, lengthy, and intimate conversation, I am definitely still a work in progress. As to telephones, thank God for e-mail.

Making It Work

Unlike periods of devotion, discipline, vacation, or games, communication is not an event but a process. Families are always in the communication process, either verbal or nonverbal. In relation to our wives and children, there are essentially six messages in every communication:

- what you intend to say
- what you actually say
- what you think you said
- what your child (wife) wants to hear
- what your child (wife) hears
- what your child (wife) thinks he or she heard

If we can harmonize all six versions of the message, then the communication process is in good shape. Dads who want to communicate well build in a feedback factor to make sure all the messages operate on the same wavelength. If you want to keep family relationships smooth, you need to keep constant vigil against distortions of the message. Let's take a look at some simple ways to improve your communication in the family:

- Be courteous and considerate.
- Cultivate the practice of listening.

- Use positive words rather than negative words if possible.
- Give praise whenever you can.
- Clearly demonstrate your expectation of results.
- Listen carefully to feedback.

Don't talk to your kids; communicate with them. As you exchange meaning, you will gain understanding. And that will be something to talk about!

Questions for Discussion

1. Evaluate your nonverbal communication (tone of voice, facial expressions, body language, etc.). Are you communicating anything negative to your children? If you're brave enough, ask your wife about it.
2. In what ways do you communicate God's Word to your children? Do you have family devotions together? Do you read and memorize the Bible together?
3. Talk about the results of parenting that you anticipate. What end product do you desire? Have you ever told your children what you hope for them?
4. How do you provide opportunities for feedback from your children?

Father/Child Dialogue

1. Dad, fight the statistics. Don't be a father who spends a few shabby minutes each day with his children. Set aside a specific time (evening meal, bedtime, weekend) to talk with your kids. Ask them to give you a list of things that they would like to talk about.
2. Kids, remember Dad is not an expert. Probably no one ever taught him to be a dad. When he makes the effort to communicate with you, try to give him more than a one-word answer. Just for fun, try asking him about *his* day.

nine

Lessons from an Old Man

Attribute: Holiness
Text: 1 Peter 1:15–17
Characters: Eli and Sons

The strength of a man consists in finding out the way God is going, and going that way.

Henry Ward Beecher

Once while playing in a golf tournament, Lee Trevino was hit by lightning out on the course. Shaken up but not seriously injured, Trevino was asked what he learned from the experience. He replied, "When God wants to play through, you'd better let him."

Well, God wants to play through. Not just to be in front of us but literally to play through us in the game of life and fathering. Of all the attributes of God discussed in this book, holiness may be the most difficult to replicate in our own lives. But Peter could not be clearer when he says to all who read his first epistle, "Just as he who called you is holy, so be holy in all you do; for it is written: 'Be holy, because I am holy'" (1 Peter 1:15–16). Peter quotes a variety of Old Testament texts here in this epistle but puts this one right smack in a fathering passage because the next verse (v. 17) says, "Since you call on a Father who judges each man's work impartially, live your lives as strangers here in reverent fear." The holiness of our heavenly Father motivates us to father our children in holy reverence.

Holy Men Lead in Difficult Times

The 1 Peter passage serves as a great springboard back into the Old Testament and the early chapters of 1 Samuel. Here we find perhaps the darkest time in the history of Israel, between slavery in Egypt and captivity in Assyria and Babylon. In the late twelfth century B.C., chaos and confusion ruled and the morale of the people was beaten into the very ground they walked on. The events of chapters 1–4 take place at Shiloh, about twenty miles north of Jerusalem, the location of the tabernacle during these ancient times. To understand the connection of Old Testament books, we need to lift Ruth from between Judges and 1 Samuel and read Judges 21:25 as an introduction to 1 Samuel: "In those days Israel had no king; everyone did as he saw fit." We add to that 1 Samuel 3:1, which tells us, "In those days the word of the LORD was rare; there were not many visions." We sense the spiritual, cultural, and political doldrums into which Samuel was born.

But Samuel is not our spotlight character for this chapter—that dubious honor falls to Eli, the old priest presiding at Shiloh. Like us, he led in difficult days. And while the twelfth century B.C. seems light-years away from our cyberspace culture in the twenty-first century, the task of Eli can be legitimately compared to the task of fathers today. Eli's failure in that role rises from the ashes of history to stare us in the face. Certainly Eli had no problem understanding God's holiness; the Bible never challenges the old priest's righteousness. But he could not reproduce the holiness, which God reflected in his life, in his evil sons, Hophni and Phinehas.

Yes, holy men lead in difficult times and they do so by God's appointment. In these difficult times to which God has called us, we can't duck the leadership responsibility either at home or at church.

Holy Men Serve by God's Appointment

Eli had not usurped the priesthood in Israel; he was a legitimate high priest from the line of Ithamar, Aaron's youngest son. We all take pride in our work, our titles, our achievements, and the respect of our professional peers, but God's primary appointment for fathers is at home not on the job. Fathering is a vocation not a pastime. Too many men fall into the trap sprung by failure at home that often drives them deeper into job involvement where they feel more confident and successful.

Some sociologists have suggested an inverse relationship between our confidence in the fathering role and the age of our children, whereas at work our confidence grows along with our years on the job. During the first eighteen months of a child's life, we burst with pride and wonderment. Then we begin to sense the reality of potential disaster somewhere around age two. Some men progressively withdraw, allowing their wives to take charge of matters as their parenting decreases.

Meanwhile, at work they enjoy promotion after promotion, salary increase after salary increase; and with all that comes more confidence. This interesting piece of research doesn't apply to every family, of course, but it does explain why some men proudly pass around pictures of preschool children but, ten or fifteen years later, never mention the struggles of handling teenagers.

Eli's story provides no solution, just a warning. Eli was a leader in difficult times and he served by God's appointment. God said to Eli, "I chose your father out of all the tribes of Israel to be my priest, to go up to my altar, to burn incense, and to wear an ephod in my presence" (1 Sam. 2:28). God says to us, "I chose you to be a father and a priest, to lead your children to my altar and to teach them about my presence in your family." You can't run from that appointment, and you can't hide from it.

W. A. Criswell, a famous Southern Baptist pastor now in heaven, tells about a time when as a seminary student he attended a Paderewski concert in Louisville, Kentucky. The house was packed, but he found one seat in the front row, right next to a beautiful girl—a double win. They stood up to stretch when the houselights came on for intermission, so he turned to the young lady and said, "Isn't this the biggest congregation you've ever seen?" No, you can't hide it. And as Eli found out, you can't run away from it. *God calls Christian fathers to lead in difficult days because they serve by God's appointment.*

Holy Men Take Responsibility for Their Children

One of my favorite school stories is about a third grader who walked up to his teacher's desk one morning to announce, "Miss Morgan, I don't want to frighten you, but my daddy says if my grades don't improve, somebody's going to get a spanking." Perhaps, but not Miss Morgan. And if spankings are called for because of a child's bad behavior, God will not look for a pastor or a youth director to do it. He'll find the child's father. That's exactly what he did with Eli.

We don't have space here to print all the verses, but we suggest you read again 1 Samuel 2:12–29, where we learn the following unsettling facts about Eli's family:

- Eli's sons didn't know the Lord (v. 12).
- Eli's sons committed robbery (vv. 13–17).
- Eli's sons fornicated at the tabernacle (v. 22).
- Eli's sons were completely undisciplined (v. 25).
- Eli honored his sons more than God (v. 29).

Here was a "holy man" raising wicked children—a situation not completely unknown in our day. Abraham Lincoln once said, "I believe the Bible is the best gift God has ever given to man. All the good from the Savior of the world is communicated to us through this Book." But Lincoln died long ago, and such talk is hardly the modern way of thinking.

In our contemporary culture, children enter schools with more secular baggage than ever before, and the load gets bigger with every week. Experiences have come to them secondhand, rather like sitting in front of a television set watching a sunset scene while the actual sun sets outside. Their culture has taught them to value speed over reflection, graphics over argument, marketing over principle, hardware over interpersonal relationships, and doing over being. Everything must be quicker, faster, farther, and sooner.

But holiness takes time, and somehow in the harried, hassled world of parenting, we fathers must demonstrate and communicate the process of seeking God and pass our search on to our children.

So holy men who lead in difficult days serve by God's appointment and bear responsibility for their own children. As we said, you can't run from or hide from it—and you can't fake it. In the city of Joliet, Illinois, a pickup truck left a burglary scene and, as a getaway maneuver, stopped at St. John the Baptist Catholic Church. It happened to be during the service and the congregation was praying. The police had no problem locating the truck but, as they went into the sanctuary, they preferred not to disturb the worshipers by creating a fuss. So they simply walked up and down the aisles.

No luck. None of the worshipers looked like a burglar. Finally, just before leaving, they decided to ask the priest, who mumbled a reply the officers could not understand. About that time they noticed he wasn't wearing a priestly collar and that two suede cowboy boots protruded from under his long black robe. You can't fake it. Faking fathers are father failures—like Eli.

We would all agree that fathers who neglect their children because they work sixteen hours a day making millions of dollars to buy large estates and yachts do not glorify God, do not practice holiness, and invite God's judgment on their lives. We might be more lenient with a pastor or priest who spends so much time "in the Lord's work" that his own children choose the wide path to destruction. *We* might, but not God. He held Eli personally responsible for the godless behavior of Hophni and Phinehas. And before this story ends, Eli is dead, both sons are dead, Israel has faced horrendous defeat by the Philistines, and the ark of the Covenant is captured. Just when you thought things couldn't get worse, that's exactly what happened.

Holy Men Hold the Church's Reputation in Their Hands

God has little interest in our excuses, yet we seem to concoct them with ease. Have a look at this list of excuses actually written by parents to teachers to explain their child's absence from the classroom.

My son is under the doctor's care and should not take physical education today—please execute him.

Please excuse my son's tardiness. I forgot to wake him up and I did not find him until I started making the beds.

Sally won't be in school a week from Friday; we have to attend a funeral.

Irresponsible parents produce irresponsible children, and the fact that Eli was a priest cut him no slack with God.

About this time we can imagine that the Hophni/Phinehas account is making some readers with adult children feel guilty. What if you made every effort to raise your kids according to biblical standards, and they have walked away from God? Whose fault is it? Throughout most of the Old Testament, the Jews functioned according to a proverb that God never gave them. It appears in Ezekiel 18:2: "The fathers eat sour grapes, and the children's teeth are set on edge." In actuality, the principle mocks God's righteous judgment and at the same time expresses self-pity and fatalism. Bad things happened to good people, and the sins of the fathers did at times seem to be visited on the sons. But Jeremiah predicted the end of this nonsense, and Ezekiel declared the old proverb null and void, replaced by the principle "The soul who sins is the one who will die" (v. 4).

To put it plainly, God holds parents responsible for the behavior of their children during the years they live at home. We assume in general that means until they head off for college or some kind of career or until they become adults. After that we may grieve, we may weep, we may pray about their failures, but the responsibility rule no longer applies. Some Christian fathers need to put the past behind them.

In his book *Lee: The Last Years*, Charles B. Flood tells about a story of General Lee visiting the home of a Kentucky lady after the war. The house was ruined and the yard scarred beyond repair. At the front of the house stood a once stately oak tree with its trunk and limbs nearly eliminated by artillery fire. The woman announced to Lee how the tree had become a monument to the aggression of the North and how she would let it stand forever as a symbol of her hatred and defiance. Lee's advice: "Cut it down, madam, and forget it."[1]

When we say that holy men hold the church's reputation in their hands, we're talking about the behavior of their children during the time they can control them (1 Tim. 3:4–5). But someone will say, Hophni and Phinehas were certainly full-grown adults when God brought judgment on Eli. Right. But they were once children, and then young boys, and the full application of the story argues that Eli did nothing along the way to produce holiness in his own sons.

Holy Men Serve with Great Risk and Great Opportunity

God gave Eli a second chance. Hophni and Phinehas may have placed themselves beyond spiritual retrieval, but God put Samuel under Eli's care, and this time the priest came through. Eli's success with Samuel did not alleviate the inevitable judgment on him, his sons, and the nation because of his prior failures, but it did leave Israel a godly priest and prophet. In an amazing sequel, however, Samuel reproduced his mentor's most tragic error. Apparently Eli taught Samuel well in all matters of public worship and personal godliness, but he could not teach him how to raise godly sons. First Samuel 8 tells us about Samuel's family. "His sons did not walk in his ways. They turned aside after dishonest gain and accepted bribes and perverted justice" (v. 3). The lives of Samuel, Hophni, and Phinehas overlapped for only a short time, but during those years Eli lived out both the risk and the opportunity of holy fathering.

You won't find holiness on a shelf at the hardware store or in the halftime show at the football game. Christian dads have to make their way through all the shallow thinking and downright heresy we and our children face every day. What children watch on television, what they read in books, what they hear from their friends, and yes, sometimes even what they hear at school must be funneled through a filter of biblical godliness. On this we might take a tip from Dr. Seuss:

My uncle ordered popovers
From the restaurant's bill of fare.

And, when they were served,
He regarded them with a penetrating stare.

Then he spoke great Words of Wisdom
As he sat there on that chair:

"To eat these things," said my uncle,
"You must exercise great care.

You may swallow down what's solid but . . .
YOU MUST SPIT OUT THE AIR!"

And as you partake of the world's bill of fare,
That's darn good advice to follow.

Do a lot of spitting out the hot air.
And be careful what you swallow.[2]

Jeff's Story

I have a vivid recollection of the day this issue of holiness burned its mark on my heart. At home with our firstborn daughter, Lyndsey, on my day off, I had the television tuned to a program unacceptable for children. Unfortunately, such unholy diversions easily find their way into our Christian homes.

As I watched, my little toddler suddenly quit playing with her toys on the floor and began to watch with me. Though I knew that she could not comprehend the words or meanings or innuendoes coming from that box, I suddenly felt the extreme conviction of a father in the process of polluting his own child! I came face-to-face with the reality that my own holiness or lack thereof would have a direct influence on my beloved child.

As I switched off the TV that day, God turned on a desire in my heart to protect my eyes and heart from the pollution of the world so that I would not bring such garbage into our home where it could spoil my children.

I certainly cannot say that I have lived a completely holy life in front of my children since that day, but the desire for family holiness has influenced many decisions during my fifteen years of fathering.

Kenn's Story

For too many years as a teenager and a young adult I equated holiness with perfection—its biblical meaning had completely eluded me. Reading Tozer's *The Knowledge of the Holy* helped, but I didn't really get a handle on personal holiness until I worked my way through Lewis Sperry Chafer's *He That Is Spiritual* and Francis Schaeffer's *True Spirituality*.[3]

The key is to value *relative* holiness with the full awareness that we'll never achieve *absolute* holiness until we get to heaven. But in our own lives and in our families, we want to raise the bar as high as possible, get rid of those lame excuses, and hold ourselves, our wives, and our children accountable to the standards of God. And that doesn't happen overnight. Sanctification involves becoming more like God and therefore more able to reproduce his character in our children.

Making It Work

So how do we avoid the Eli syndrome? Let's try a three-C approach—*confession, commitment,* and *consistency.*

- We acknowledge our past sins and trust God to forgive us.
- We confess to our wives and our children where we have let them down on the matter of reflecting God's holiness in our behavior and in our dealings with them.
- We commit first to God, then to our families, that by his grace things will be different from now on.
- We trust the Holy Spirit to produce consistency of holy living in our life so that our children can see over time what

it means to trust God, to depend on him, and to live in the light of his standards.

According to an ancient Japanese custom, folks in that country used to take elderly people up a path to some lonely resting place where they would die. Everyone in the society accepted it; it was simply a cultural practice. One young man, horrified at the prospect of taking his mother up the death path, dropped little twigs along the way. When she questioned this strange behavior he said, "I'm doing this so you can find your way home." Christian dads are twig-droppers on the road of family destruction. We may not change society, but God expects us to rescue at least one family, and we better have our priorities straight.

Questions for Discussion

1. What could possibly have happened in Samuel's adult life to cause him to reproduce Eli's horrendous blunder with his own sons?
2. Carefully study the first chapter of 1 Peter and write down specific areas where you can begin to work immediately on personal holiness.
3. Since holiness is a rather abstract concept, what things might you do differently in your life to show your children you're trying to be holy as a reflection of God's character?

Father/Child Dialogue

1. Dad, explain holiness to your children in terms they can understand. Articulate your personal commitment to holiness in your home.
2. Kids, ask Dad what it means for you to be holy at home, at school, and out with your friends.

ten

Winning the Game

Attribute: Discipline
Text: Hebrews 12:5–11
Characters: Eli and Sons

It's easier to fight for one's principles than to live up to them.

Alfred Adler

In January of 2001 the Fox Family network aired a four-hour version of *Les Misérables*, Victor Hugo's compelling saga of man's heroic struggle against forces that threaten to break even the strongest and most noble spirits. The book became an instant success when published in 1862 and continues to capture the imagination of people around the world. The musical version still holds a prime spot among entertainment ventures of that kind.

Jean Valjean, the suffering hero of the story, depicts a man Hugo knew during his own lifetime. Claude Gueux stole a loaf of bread to feed his starving family. While in prison, he murdered one of his persecuting wardens and was executed in 1834. The character of Inspector Javert, many believe, was modeled after Victor's father, Leopold Hugo, a career army officer who eventually became a count and a general under Napoléon. Literary experts indicate that Leopold Hugo possessed the kind of obsessive behavior and "sense of duty" Javert displays until the final scene.

Discipline plays a major role in *Les Misérables*. Javert's absolute dedication to his duty as a police officer drives him far beyond the boundaries of reason and completely beyond mercy. On the positive side, however, Jean Valjean's dedication to truth, courage, and helping people in need shows disciplined behavior in scene after scene throughout the play, just as suffering one's way to salvation represents a standard theme in Catholic novels. But no character in Hugo's book depicts a biblical father carrying out spiritual discipline in a family setting. Amazingly, it's difficult to find that pattern in the Bible as well.

In the late twelfth century B.C., Israel churned in chaos. The tabernacle stood at Shiloh, twenty miles north of Jerusalem, and spiritual leadership rested in Eli's hands. The old man served by God's appointment and he served in difficult days. As we noted in chapter 9, the text tells us, "In those days the word of the LORD was rare; there were not many visions" (1 Sam. 3:1).

Eli's personal life and ministry seemed beyond reproach, but he could not handle parenting, and his weakest dimension in the family arena was his failure to discipline. The text says, "Eli's sons were wicked men; they had no regard for the LORD" (1 Sam. 2:12). In our last chapter, we saw the problem; in this chapter we explore the solutions. Perhaps the key is 1 Samuel 3:13: "For I told him that I would judge his family forever because of the sin he knew about; his sons made themselves contemptible, and he failed to restrain them." What a tragic commentary on a spiritual leader who failed in his fathering discipline!

Coach the Team

Teams are made up of captains and players who play specific positions. All players have to know exactly what the coach expects of them and what will happen if they don't fulfill their roles. Every player also has to know how to take orders from the captain or coach and to do so without rebellion or bitterness.

In the Christian family, God ordains parental captains. Failure to understand and exercise biblical roles and responsibilities in the family creates havoc with any disciplinary structure.

Imagine a football team on which the tight end lines up behind the running back or a defensive tackle insists on kicking the point after a touchdown. Making discipline work may mean going back to the basics to determine what moms do, what dads do, and what children do according to God's design for Christian families.

In the family, all the players may get a voice (depending on their ages), but the final decisions belong to the co-captains, the parents. Their task carries with it the essential process of carefully pruning the sin along with encouraging the good in their children. When punishment is meted out in anger and bitterness coupled with sarcastic words and demeaning language, it can destroy a child's spirit. Careful discipline (wisely structured rules and requirements) matched with loving punishment will show children that their wills must be submissive to their parents who, in turn, submit to the will of God.

As you prune and encourage, show children how family rules and guidelines derive from the principles of God's Word. This helps them understand that the boundaries have been set not "because I said so" (a phrase many parents revert to as a last resort) but because God said so and had good reasons. These explanations will eventually become internalized by your children, giving them the foundation to make good choices as they grow older.

Discipline means training the team. Basketball coaches talk about a player "out of control," which means he may be extremely fast, a good shot, and aggressive on defense, but he does not work with other players in a disciplined game plan. Just as in sports, discipline doesn't come automatically to children; somebody needs to run them through training camp to get them ready for the season.

Good games require fair play. Vulnerability, honesty, and integrity create a positive atmosphere of home nurture. When children cheat on the rules at school and try to get away with anything they can, they show that their parents don't require them to take seriously responsibilities at home. When parents are more lenient with one child than with others, the siblings may start to show bitterness over their enforced discipline and their sibling's excessive freedom. They wonder if their obedience has any value in the eyes of their parents. That's why the

Scripture tells parents, "Do not embitter your children, or they will become discouraged" (Col. 3:21).

Both captains have to say the same things for the same reasons and model that all-important family unity. If a child is not required to follow the rules, he or she actually does not feel a part of the family team. In truth, the parents have withheld love by refusing to enforce their guidelines. Their laxity can result in a very insecure child.

Be Conscious of the Fans

Most professional athletic teams play much better on their home field or floor for obvious reasons, but road games are important too. As parents we need to remember that people—neighbors, friends at church, relatives, teachers, and even strangers we meet in public places—are watching our little family team. On the one hand we can't be intimidated by the fact that people are watching. Yet we do remember that the Scripture says, "Since we are surrounded by such a great cloud of witnesses, . . . let us run with perseverance the race marked out for us" (Heb. 12:1). These words introduce one of the great passages of God's Word on the subject of discipline. And, once again, we find God's fatherly example portrayed for us.

Discipline is a necessary component of love (Heb. 12:5–6). The Lord disciplines those whom he loves and punishes those he receives. Obviously, parental discipline offered by Christians within the family context should always be loving—never administered in anger. Avoid irrational emotional outbursts. A loving response points out the wrong, explains the reason for the consequences, and proceeds with forgiveness.

Discipline identifies the child as a bona fide member of the family (Heb. 12:7–8). The reference to earthly fathers in these verses indicates again that God teaches us spiritual truth through family illustrations. We know we belong to the family of God because he disciplines us to bring us into line when we displease him. Uncontrolled, undisciplined children might as well not have a family.

Discipline by human parents is never perfect (Heb. 12:9–10). Scripture teaches that we are to reverence, or honor, parents who correct us, even when they do it imperfectly and sometimes at their own whims. Discipline must be accepted, even welcomed, by Christian children and teenagers because parents hold their authoritative positions by divine appointment. And, since we all know the captain sometimes makes mistakes, it may help from time to time to tell our children just that. *Discipline always seems painful at the time but produces fruit in the end* (Heb. 12:11). When the task gets discouraging, Christian parents must remember the reward. We know we're attempting to do God's will, yet sometimes our efforts at discipline and punishment seem to stir up greater rebellion and achieve negative results. Successful discipline requires patience, persistence, and keeping the end in view.

Born with no arms, Harold Wilkey required constant care and help. On one occasion, a neighbor watched while Harold struggled to put on his shirt while his mother just sat and looked at him. Exasperated, the neighbor shouted, "Why don't you help him?" Harold's mother calmly responded, "I am helping him."

Discipline does not always mean doing things to or for our children. At times it can mean requiring them to do essential things for themselves.

Control Practice Sessions

The difference between discipline and punishment seems unclear in the minds of too many coaches and parents. Punishment should be a consequence when discipline fails. Discipline erects fences; punishment comes when a player breaks down the fences or deliberately transgresses the boundaries.

Discipline Precedes Punishment

The word *discipline* flows from the root word *disciple.* Used as a noun, *disciple* means "learner" or "follower." How appropriate to describe what parents do with children in the Christian home! Discipline molds and strengthens godly character by means of structured behavioral guidelines. Wise parents control the environment toward these nurturing goals as soon as the baby comes home from the hospital. Coaching and "captaining" begin immediately.

A parent who administers punishment before the boundaries, rules, and "fences" of discipline have been established engages in unjust and unproductive behavior. It's like asking a soccer player to follow the rules without explaining them first and then kicking her out of the game when she violates one. We want nurture not negation, cultivation not confinement.

Discipline Presupposes Punishment

Only people who believe in original sin can understand this principle. Advocates of the belief that the nature of children is either good or neutral argue that children should never need punishment at all, assuming their environment is correct. But the Bible teaches that the evil sin nature is in every child's heart. Punishment, which flows out of discipline, will at times be necessary.

The overall picture of Scripture demands that Christian parents lead their children and teenagers from basic sinful, natural rebellion to a place of enforced discipline. Enforced discipline then leads to self-discipline and ultimately to Christ-discipline with lives surrendered to his lordship. Ancient wisdom works today—"Correct your son, and he will give you comfort; he will also delight your soul" (Prov. 29:17 NASB).

Discipline Prepares for Punishment

When telling our children what they can and cannot do, we must also tell them what will happen when they violate family rules. Disciplined coaches tend to produce disciplined children by the very nature of the order they bring to practice.

Think about two-year-olds who act totally uninhibited in public places. They run up and down church aisles and climb into the pews; they throw food around the table at restaurants or when the family dines at someone else's home; they seem oblivious to parental commands to "stop" or "come here" or "be quiet." What you see in public, of course, only reflects what goes on at home. These children live in worlds without fences. Their parents have not committed themselves strongly enough to erecting boundaries of behavior and letting punishment follow discipline when and where it must.

J. Paul Getty, the famous oil magnate, was once the world's richest man. To manipulate and control his children, he changed his will twenty-one times. In the process he drove one son to suicide and failed to show up at the funeral of another who died at age twelve. Here's a copy of Getty's diary entry for that day: "Funeral for darling Timmy. A sad day. Send cable to Zone that Aminoil can have fifty percent of Eocenle by giving us fifty percent of Burgen and paying ten cents per barrel handling." You may not be as rich as Getty, but you can still make the same mistakes by prioritizing your business over your family.

Unity between the co-captains helps the process significantly. Young children learn to pit Mom against Dad to get what they want when the parents don't support each other. When disagreements occur over disciplinary matters, parents must stick together for the public moment, then hash out the issues in private. Parents must periodically sit down together—and with the children as they grow older—to refine guidelines for behavior and consequences for lapses. Angry scenes between parent and child can fade into distant memory when rules have been agreed on ahead of time.

It takes time and effort to decide what we will allow our children to do and what we will not tolerate. Sure it seems harsh to firmly stop that little hand reaching repeatedly for the breakable vase on the coffee table or playfully yanking the eyeglasses off Grandma's face. But remember: That firm stop is at the same time a punishment that can be understood by a very young child and a part of the network of behavior we create to guide him or her toward a satisfactory lifestyle.

In a wonderful song called "Broken Pieces," Steve and Annie Chapman remind us to get a firm grip on our parenting responsibility and especially on the crucial behavior of discipline.

> All across the nation homes are falling
> And daily the number increases
> And the ones who suffer most aren't the mothers and the
> fathers
> The children are the broken pieces.

The children are the broken pieces when a home falls apart
The children are the broken pieces; whose gonna mend their
  hearts?
And when a nation is filled with broken pieces
No one can build among the ruins
You mothers and you fathers if you will not stay together
Your children pay the price for what you're doing.
God come and mend the broken pieces.[1]

Jeff's Story

My children have grown up playing soccer, a game I never played much as a kid because my peers didn't consider it "cool" back then. But in watching my children play the game, I have discovered that soccer requires a great deal of discipline. As Soccer Pals, our kids joined the other munchkins on the field chasing the ball everywhere it went, despite the coach's pleas from the sideline, "Don't bunch up!"

But now my children have learned the discipline of soccer. They play their positions; they pass the ball; they work as a team. And more important, they are learning the discipline of living. They don't just run with the pack or wander anywhere they please. They play their positions in the family and contribute to the success of the team. Disciplined families know how to work together so that everyone wins.

Kenn's Story

Our two children were very different in their temperaments. Parents with three, four, or more say it doesn't matter how many children you have; each one develops a unique personality.

Jeff was sensitive and easily corrected. Because of his tender spirit, a cross word or stern look would often straighten out his improper behavior. When the house was quiet, we could probably find him sitting on the floor surrounded by toys or reading a book.

Julie was another case altogether. During her preschool years, a quiet house told us we had better check on her whereabouts. She was often found eating the dirt from a flowerpot or pulling all the toilet paper off the roll and making a pretty pile on the floor. Our approach to correction with her required greater firmness and regularity.

Making It Work

There is no one *right* way to handle discipline or punishment. There are, however, several clearly wrong ways, especially physical violence and demeaning name-calling. An occasional spanking, *never done in parental anger,* may prove necessary. We deplore anything hinting of child abuse; abused children often grow into abusive parents. If, as a parent, you find yourself struggling with uncontrollable anger and inappropriate punishment, we encourage you to seek professional help. A child brought up in fear of parental temper tantrums (much more damaging from parents than from children) will have a very difficult time placing trust in God for ultimate matters.

Several practical fathering behaviors flow out of our study of Hebrews 12:

- Never lose sight of sin as the ultimate culprit in a child's negative behavior.
- Remember that the key is not perpetual success but faithful effort.
- Expect pain at the moment of punishment and look for righteousness and peace later.
- Map out a straight road for your family and get a grip on those feeble arms and weak knees (v. 12).
- Don't give up on spiritually lame children (v. 13).

The best discipline approach designs each individual rule and treats each situation with the goal of applying biblical principles to your family. May no one ever write about you, "He failed to restrain his children."

Questions for Discussion

1. In what specific ways can Christian parents develop orderly disciplined patterns with young children? With young teens? With older teens?
2. Do you believe in physical punishment? What forms are most helpful? How do you handle the various biblical texts (notably Proverbs) that seem to affirm the value of physical punishment?
3. Why is it important for husband and wife to present a united front in dealing with the matters of discipline and punishment? How can they best do that?

Father/Child Dialogue

1. Dad, tell your kids about the disciplinary measures your parents used and why they were effective or ineffective. Be sure to do it without putting Grandma and Grandpa in a bad light.
2. Kids, think about one way your dad disciplines you. Tell him how that discipline helps you obey.

eleven

Find Us Faithful

Attribute: Faithfulness
Text: Psalm 146:5–9
Character: Elkanah

> Try not to become a man of success but rather try to become a man of value.
>
> Albert Einstein

With a deep breath in his lungs and a firm grasp on his courage, Mark is about to take on the biggest job of his life. At the age of twenty-eight he's getting married. Some people would jokingly say he is *finally* getting married, but to Mark everything leading up to his wedding with Teri fits the careful plan of God. Soon, talk must become action and the jokes about bachelorhood and marriage must be put behind him. The demands of his sky-rocketing career in electronics research must now take second place to the priorities of his role as a faithful husband and per-haps soon a faithful father.

Only now is Mark beginning to understand how much more learning he has to do. To become a *discipler*, he must first be a *disciple*. To become a teacher, he first must learn. He and Teri both come from families in which fathers lived out decades of faithfulness to their wives and their children, and Mark has no intention of blemishing that record.

He reads newspapers and watches television, so he knows the distorted image of fathering displayed by twenty-first-century media. The only place he can view faithful fathering anymore is on late-night reruns of *The Waltons* or *Little House on the Prairie.* Mark also knows the staggering statistics coming out of national polls. A Harris poll indicated that 84 percent of Americans believe the family is important, but two out of five want no children and only 25 percent want a "stable sex life." Fewer than half the people responding to the survey indicated they would "work at marriage." Still another study showed that American seventh and eighth graders average seven and a half minutes per week of focused conversation with their fathers. Still another study showed that fathers of preschoolers spend an average of thirty-seven seconds a day talking with their children.

So Mark knows the pitfalls. And he's determined not to be a statistic but a father, a faithful father who understands that God's immutability forms a foundation for faith in a world marked by constant change. Mark's experiences with his heavenly Father have always shown that God's faithfulness is completely reliable, the ultimate Rock in a very shaky world. He knows the truth of Psalm 146:5–6:

> Blessed is he whose help is the God of Jacob,
>   whose hope is in the LORD his God,
> the Maker of heaven and earth,
>   the sea, and everything in them—
>   the LORD, who remains faithful forever.

The faithful heavenly Father is the one who sustains the fatherless and the widow (v. 9). So Mark has not only determined to be a faithful father, he has actually identified areas that will be the focus of his daily prayer and his lifestyle.

Faithfulness in Leading

In a day when *leadership* means visibility, popularity, likeability, and drive, Mark wants to be a quiet family leader who doesn't need constant high-profile activity to mark his role in the home. That's the kind of leader Elkanah was back in the twelfth century B.C. We have already visited this era in the last few chapters and we know the evils that occurred at the tabernacle in Shiloh.

Back in the hill country of Ephraim, Elkanah and Hannah struggled with her barrenness. Actually, Elkanah had two wives, not uncommon in the cultural patterns of Israel at that time. He married Hannah first, and when she could not conceive a child, he married Peninnah, who did bear children. We have seen this in Abraham's wives and Jacob's wives and we know God never designed this plan but allowed a loophole in the overall pattern.

Both Elkanah and Hannah were deeply devoted followers of Jehovah, but it was a tough time to maintain that role. Organized religion was stagnant; cultic practices dominated the culture; pagan behavior clamored for attention everywhere. Actually, it sounds rather like the twenty-first century.

Yet Elkanah led his family in faithful worship. "Year after year this man went up from his town to worship and sacrifice to the LORD Almighty at Shiloh" (1 Sam. 1:3). Hannah had wisely married a faithful man, and they had a great relationship. The text tells us, "To Hannah he gave a double portion because he loved her, and the LORD had closed her womb" (v. 5). "Elkanah her husband would say to her, 'Hannah, why are you weeping? Why don't you eat? Why are you downhearted? Don't I mean more to you than ten sons?' " (v. 8).

When God answered their prayers by giving them Samuel, faithful Elkanah supported his wife's vow, "When the man Elkanah went up with all his family to offer the annual sacrifice to the LORD and to fulfill his vow, Hannah did not go. . . . Elkanah her husband told her, 'Stay here until you have weaned him; only may the LORD make good his word' " (vv. 21–23). Though Hannah usually receives all the press for her passionate prayer at the tabernacle, Elkanah fully supported her difficult decision to give Samuel back to the Lord.

Faithfulness in biblical fathering requires recognition of the headship role, much disputed in recent decades. The Greek word *kephale* (head) appears fifty-eight times in the New Testament to describe a part of human anatomy and thirteen times as a symbol for leadership. Faithful leadership is the other side of submission—it makes submission possible. Despite many modern interpretations of a variety of biblical texts, conservative evangelical scholars still acknowledge the God-ordained leadership of husbands and fathers in their own homes (1 Cor. 11:3, 8–9; Eph. 5:23; 1 Peter 3:1). Spiritually mature men understand this not as dominance but responsibility. In one of his books, Gordon McDonald likened it to sitting at the back of a canoe, responsible for steering its direction and making sure you look ahead for dangerous logs or rocks in the river. All this reflects the faithfulness of the heavenly Father. In relation to both God and us, the Greek and Hebrew words mean that men following God's pattern will be solid, certain, dependable, and reliable (1 Cor. 1:9; 10:13; 2 Cor. 1:18). Carl Laney picks up on one of those words.

One aspect of God's faithfulness is the fact that He is totally dependable. How often have you been disappointed by people who did not fulfill what you expected of them? People are late for appointments or miss them all together. People say they have forgiven someone only to bring up the matter weeks later. People promise to help on a project and then don't follow through. People disappoint us because they are marked by weakness and sin. But God can always be counted on! You will never be disappointed when you rely on Him (Isa. 28:16; Rom. 10:11).[1]

So God models faithful leadership for us, and we model faithful leadership for everyone else in the family. Perhaps that especially relates to our sons whom, from their earliest years, we groom into the next generation of fathers and church leaders. Many years ago, before Jeff was born, Kenn's mother gave him a little poem. We have no idea of the source, but have a look at the words.

A careful man I ought to be, a little fellow follows me.
I do not dare to go astray for fear he'll go the self-same way.
I cannot once escape his eyes, whate're he sees me do he tries.
Like me he says he's going to be—the little chap that follows me.
He thinks that I am good and fine, believes in every word of mine.
The base in me he must not see—the little chap who follows me.

I must remember as I go, from summer's sun and winter's
　　snow,
I'm building for the years to be that little chap who follows me.

Some of the great men of the Bible (Jacob, Eli, David) failed
at fathering. We do not offer them as models, nor does this book
call us to father like Elkanah or Joseph, solid as they may have
been. Our task, our call from Scripture, is to father like the
Father.

Faithfulness in Loving

From the third chapter of Colossians we can distill three
essential commands for three different types of family members: "Wives, submit . . . husbands, love . . . children, obey" (Col.
3:18–20). It almost looks as though the Holy Spirit moved Paul
to reduce all his family teaching into simple sound bites nobody
could misunderstand. To put it another way, if we arranged a
list of masculine duties in the home, it would include provide,
protect, teach, lead, and a host of other responsibilities—but at
the top of the list would be *love*.

Let's get back to Mark for a moment. Because he's been single clear up to the ripe old age of twenty-eight, he has had ample
opportunity to view other marriages in action and form some
solid opinions about what he wants his family to look like. From
his analysis of the early chapters of Genesis, he has concluded
that God intentionally created companionship between a man
and a woman. To make that possible, God's game plan was to
make leadership and submission irreversible and unconditional
ways of relating.

It all goes back to the team concept we illustrated in earlier
chapters. We have stored a lot of useless basketball trivia in our
heads over the years, and one of the things we remember is that
when the Los Angeles Laker team was in its glory years (which
have recently returned), every time Magic Johnson scored thirty
or forty points, the Lakers lost! For Mark, shooting baskets
doesn't take priority; his job is to play point guard—watch the
floor, set up the plays, and pass the ball. That means he takes
the lead in developing loving relationships in the family.

Is God still our model in faithful loving? Here's Ryrie:

> The Bible directly states that "God is love" (1 John 4:8). The absence of the article before "love" (the verse does not say, God is the love) indicates that this is the very nature of God. The presence of the article before "God" (the God is love) shows that the statement is not reversible; it cannot read, "Love is God."[2]

Faithfulness in leading, faithfulness in loving—these are two-thirds of the great triangle of faithful fathering. More than a quarter century ago, a conservative Catholic columnist, Michael Novak, wrote in *Harper's* magazine:

> The role of a father or mother and of children with respect to them, is the absolutely critical center of social force. . . . One unforgettable law has been learned painfully through all the oppressions, disasters and injustices of the last thousand years— if things go well with the family, life is worth living; when the family falters, life falls apart.[3]

Faithfulness in Learning

The Bible directs the focus of teaching on Christian fathers. In fact Paul spent a good bit of time telling Titus how to teach men of any age so that they could function properly in their families and in the church. Obviously God does not need to learn and therefore does not serve as a model in this case, but the biblical information still downloads faster than we can print it out.

The Greek text of Titus 2 includes eleven words for *instruction* and the English text, thirteen. The first and last verses emphasize teaching, and the entire chapter deals with different groupings of adults. Paul told Titus to "teach the older men to be temperate, worthy of respect, self-controlled, and sound in faith, in love and in endurance" (2:2). He told Titus to teach the younger men "to be self-controlled" (2:6). Taken as a block, the information in the Old and New Testaments puts us behind a huge learning curve to keep up with both sides of the equation— learning so that we can teach.

We learn in order to teach our wives (1 Cor. 14:35): In reality, of course, many Christian wives know a good bit more about the Bible than their husbands, mainly because they attend more church services and read their Bibles more frequently. But reality does not always reflect what should be, especially when we apply scriptural measures to our behavior.

We learn in order to teach our children (Deut. 6:1–9): Sunday school, children's church, Awana, youth camp, Bible quizzing, and a host of other activities for children and young people are only a *support*, not a *substitute*, for our own fatherly role as mentors.

We learn in order to teach at our churches (2 Tim. 3:16–17): About twenty years ago a church that we both attended began an elder training program. Each of the nine elders serving the congregation at that time took a mentee who was willing to acknowledge that he did not yet meet the qualifications of eldership but wanted sincerely to move in that direction. A young insurance salesman with a wonderful wife and two lovely daughters entered the program. He was summoned to the home office of his company and interviewed for a major promotion. The vice president of personnel asked him dozens of questions, among which he included, "What is your greatest goal in life?" The young man thought about that for a while and then said simply, "I want to be considered worthy by my church to be an elder."

That response speaks volumes about faithfulness in learning. Yes, he could have said he wanted to be the greatest father in the world, but the reference to eldership assumes biblical behavior at home. Oh, to have seen that vice president's face when he heard what surely must have been a rather unique answer to a typical question!

Jeff's Story

I can best demonstrate my dad's faithfulness to me by describing his dedicated attendance at my high school basketball games. All four years, whether I gathered splinters on the bench or made the starting lineup, my dad attended nearly every home game and even many away games. He cheered our team, counseled the coaches, advised the referees, and always encouraged me. Though my dad shouldered heavy responsibilities as a Bible college president at the time, he faithfully supported his son's basketball habit. So I define fatherly faithfulness as *being there*.

Kenn's Story

Sometimes we must look to God as a model of faithfulness because there is no one else. I have already mentioned that my own father was spiritually, maritally, and physically unfaithful. I determined long before Jeff was born that I should act toward him in exactly the opposite way that my father had acted toward me. The constant awareness of the faithfulness of God has been a strength throughout my entire life. We hear a lot of talk about surrogate fathers; that's exactly what the King of heaven has been to me.

Making It Work

Even as we say the word *faithfulness*, we understand that it obviously comes from the same root as the word *faith*. Actually, the same Greek word *(pistis)* can be translated either way and comes from a verb meaning to *believe* or *trust*. To put it another way, faithfulness depends on faith. Strong-willed determination and dramatic effort cannot get the job done. We can be faithful only when God activates our faith to the level of overt behavior. Our faith in God enables us to have faith in our family and loyal commitment to each member.

So how do we develop faithfulness in leadership, love, and learning?

- Make sure that you have been born again, that you have trusted Jesus Christ for your salvation.
- Allow the Holy Spirit to govern your attitudes, words, and behavior with your wife and children.
- Take the lead in family worship and in bringing the family to public worship.

- Ask God to give you the courage to stand up for your Lord on the job (and be faithful as an employee as well).
- Set an example of the control Paul talked about when he wrote to Titus.

In 1987 Jon Mohr wrote the words and music for a song titled "Find Us Faithful" based on 1 Corinthians 4:2. It seems to fit right here.

> Oh, may all who come behind us find us faithful;
> May the fire of our devotion light their way.
> May the footprints that we leave lead them to believe,
> And the lives we live inspire them to obey.
> Oh, may all who come behind us find us faithful.[4]

May our children find us to be faithful fathers who walk in step with our faithful Father.

Questions for Discussion

1. In which of the three areas (leading, loving, learning) do you feel your faithfulness is the strongest? How about the weakest?
2. Make a list of the areas in your life in which you might be (or have been) tempted to be unfaithful.
3. What might you need to change in your life to more effectively teach your wife and children?

Father/Child Dialogue

1. Dad, promise your kids you will be faithful to them and to their mom and make sure they understand exactly what that means.
2. Kids, write your dad a note thanking him for some aspect of his faithfulness to you.

twelve

A Gift from God

Attribute: Wisdom
Text: Romans 11:33
Characters: Solomon and Sons

Committing a great truth to memory is admirable; committing it to life is wisdom.

William A. Ward

At Dallas Seminary it is the annual practice at the end of the spring semester to invite the four best homiletics students among graduating seniors to speak in chapel during what is called Senior Preaching Week. In 1980 one nominee chose a message on God, intending to speak about the primary attributes of the heavenly Father. He managed to approach the pulpit, grasp the edges firmly, and say to the assembled crowd, "This theme is too great for me." Apparently he told the truth, for at that precise moment he passed out, fell backward, and landed in the arms of then academic dean Dr. Don Campbell.

Though we don't plan any surprise landings, we feel that way about this entire book. The theme of applying God's attributes to human fathering has caused us to struggle over each chapter, perhaps never more deeply than in this chapter about *wisdom*.

In 1 Kings 3:28 the Bible says of Solomon, "When all Israel heard the verdict the king had given, they held the king in awe, because they saw that he had wisdom from God to administer justice." This famous narrative of Solomon's wise judgment of two mothers pinpoints precisely what we need in our families—wisdom from God to administer justice. And we know that comes from God because James says, "If any of you lacks wisdom, he should ask God, who gives generously to all without finding fault, and it will be given to him" (James 1:5). God alone controls the deep well of wisdom, as Paul poetically describes: "Oh, the depth of the riches of the wisdom and knowledge of God! How unsearchable his judgments, and his paths beyond tracing out!" (Rom. 11:33).

One practical way to think about wisdom is to picture it as the application of knowledge. Not everyone with knowledge has wisdom, but everyone with wisdom certainly has knowledge. As A. W. Tozer puts it:

> Wisdom, among other things, is the ability to devise perfect ends and to achieve those ends by the most perfect means. It sees the end from the beginning, so there can be no need to guess or conjecture. Wisdom sees everything in focus, each in proper relationship to all, and is thus able to work toward predestined goals with flawless precision.[1]

Wow! If we could just capture 1 percent of that description in our own lives and families. That one paragraph points out the essential growth pattern of wisdom that we all should desire.

Our family portrait for this chapter centers on Solomon and his many sons. Obviously, we cannot focus on results, since the kingdom came unglued despite Solomon's great wisdom. Nevertheless, Solomon certainly gets an A for effort, especially his fatherly advice in the Book of Proverbs. Remember, neither a promise nor precept, a proverb is simply a short, poignant phrase with meaning that can apply in many situations. Proverbs offer lessons by reflecting on the way things and people relate to right values and right conduct.

The Bible calls us to fear God and behave in ways that please him. Let's zero in on the "don't forget" section of Proverbs 3. The lesson on wisdom here lies within a context that admonishes us to follow wisdom's guidelines in relationships with God and other people. What kinds of things must we fathers remember in order to activate the lessons of this passage? Here are a series of negative imperatives to help plant this theme in our heart and family.

Don't Forget My Teaching

What would happen if we started every day by telling our children what Solomon does in verses 1 and 2 of Proverbs 3?

> Do not forget my teaching,
> but keep my commands in your heart,
> for they will prolong your life many years
> and bring you prosperity.

We certainly believe that children who obey godly parents will live better lives than those who do not. We affirm that children who receive biblical teaching at home and implement what they learn should enjoy happier lives before God than those who had no such privilege or those who rebel against it.

Unless we remember, however, that this is a proverb, not a promise, we could easily fall victim to what has been called in recent years "prosperity gospel." Yes, quite often the righteous are prosperous and happy (Prov. 12:21), but the Bible teaches that wicked people also enjoy strength and prosperity (Ps. 73:3, 12). So we cannot teach our children that if they obey God's Word, they will have material prosperity. Nevertheless, it is the responsibility of fathers (along with mothers) to create a value system that gives children the opportunity to live rich and fruitful lives before God.

Of course kids know proverbs too. In one of those crazy messages that proliferate on the Internet, we found the following "Kids' Advice to Kids."

- Never trust a dog to watch your food.
- When your dad is mad and asks you, "Do I look stupid?" don't answer.

- When your mom is mad at your dad, don't let her brush your hair.
- Don't sneeze in front of your mother when you're eating crackers.
- Never hold a dust buster and a cat at the same time.
- You can't hide a piece of broccoli in a glass of milk.
- If you want a kitten, start out by asking for a horse.
- Never try to baptize a cat.

These great words of wisdom, allegedly drawn from children between the ages of nine and twelve, remind us that we have a bigger job than we thought. We notice too how many of those childish admonitions spring out of relationships with parents. Yes, we want moral character well established in our children, but it must also be found in their parents. Only when we reflect what we teach will the lessons really get through to the hearts of our children.

Many parents have selected Christian schools or home schooling for their children because they have been crushed by the way some public schools beat down the parental wisdom they have carefully attempted to convey at home. God must give us grace and persistence in encouraging our children to remember the truth and faith we have taught them and in helping them assume appropriate biblical roles.

Don't Forget to Be Loving and Faithful

Proverbs 3:3–4 gives another admonition followed by a reward:

> Let love and faithfulness never leave you;
>   bind them around your neck, write them on the tablet of
>   your heart.
> Then you will win favor and a good name
>   in the sight of God and man.

Love and *faithfulness* served as two basic covenant terms in ancient Israel. The word for *love* here refers to the kind of obligations one incurs in a relationship. *Faithfulness* reflects precisely how we would use the English word today—reliability, stability, and trust. Daily we model for our children such a life of loving faithfulness. The metaphors of *binding* them around our neck and *writing* them on our heart remind us that these godly graces should be both internal and external. Internally we can be loving and faithful because God writes that kind of behavior on our heart through the Holy Spirit. Outwardly we wear love and faithfulness like a snappy necktie, adorning our appearance, not through pride in the possession but in the loved One who gave it.

Jennifer Berman, in her book *Why Dogs Are Better than Kids,* offers several reasons for her title. No doubt at times we wonder if our wisdom isn't more suited to raising dogs than children.

- It doesn't take forty-five minutes to get a dog ready to go out in the winter.
- Dogs cannot lie.
- Dogs never resist nap time.
- You don't need to get extra phone lines for a dog.
- Dogs don't pester you about getting a kid.
- Dogs don't care if the peas have been touched by the mashed potatoes.
- Dogs are housebroken by the time they are twelve weeks old.
- Your dog is not embarrassed if you sing in public.
- If your dog is a bad seed, your genes cannot be blamed.[2]

Don't get discouraged. As love and faithfulness flow out from you, God will etch his wisdom on the hearts of your children. The dog might even benefit too!

Don't Forget to Trust the Lord

Solomon continues by saying:

> Trust in the LORD with all your heart
> and lean not on your own understanding;

> in all your ways acknowledge him,
> and he will make your paths straight.
>
> Proverbs 3:5–6

These verses of chapter 3 build a logical progression, an argument for a wise and godly lifestyle. If our children expect long life and prosperity along with a good reputation with God and people, they cannot assume that human understanding, however highly developed through education and experience, can achieve the elusive goal. They must totally depend on the Lord for everything. We parents have exactly the same need.

Just a few years ago, Kenn struggled with the agonizing death of a friend. For reasons known only to God, a young wife and mother of two children, actively involved in ministry and continuously reflecting Jesus Christ, was snatched to heaven. For months we watched her suffer and finally watched her die. At the memorial service, several testified of her stubborn trust in the Savior before the illness, during the illness, and right to the time of death. We find no human understanding to rely on in such a painful situation. An experience like that makes us want to scream at the heavens and ask God if he really knows what he's doing.

When that scream, vocal or silent, reaches the gates of glory, the Father directs our hearts to a passage like this. No exceptions—in *all* your ways acknowledge him and your path will be straight. We're all walking commercials for God's grace; he has signed his name on our lives, often in the dark red ink of pain. Second Corinthians 12:9 serves as a compass for godly fathers: "My grace is sufficient for you, for my power is made perfect in weakness." From the film *Shadowlands,* we hear C. S. Lewis reminding us, "God whispers to us in our pleasures; God speaks to us in our consciousness; God shouts to us in our pain. It is his megaphone to a deaf world."

Don't Forget to Fear the Lord

Some young Christian dads, still lacking experience and wisdom, seem like wise guys intent on portraying a macho image,

which in the long run betrays spiritual wisdom. Solomon deals
with that in Proverbs 3:7–8:

> Do not be wise in your own eyes;
> fear the LORD and shun evil.
> This will bring health to your body
> and nourishment to your bones.

So there is a reward to following righteousness—health and
nourishment. In the context of Proverbs, healing may be spiritual and emotional, though certainly those who walk circum-
spectly before God can experience better physical health as
well.

Once again, however, a warning seems in order. Interpreting
Scripture like this as a promise of health, either for ourselves or
for our children, mishandles the text and leads to improper con-
clusions. After acknowledging the general statement of the
proverb, we have to recognize that many very sick people fear
the Lord and shun evil. *The presence or absence of health and
wealth in our lives does not accurately reflect our relationship with
God.* The proverb only affords a generalization.

Earlier we mentioned the death of a godly young woman. On
January 20, 1994, George Burns celebrated his ninety-eighth
birthday by entertaining a sellout crowd at Caesar's Palace in
Las Vegas. What a contrast! Does God really know what he's
doing? Does the world really need George Burns and not godly
young mothers who reflect Jesus to their children? We have no
human understanding for such a dilemma. As with many things
we face in our fathering role, we throw ourselves back on the
wisdom of verse 5: "Trust in the LORD with all your heart and
lean not on your own understanding."

Don't Forget to Give

How could wisdom possibly be connected with generosity?
Here it is, right in our passage:

> Honor the LORD with your wealth,
> with the firstfruits of all your crops;

then your barns will be filled to overflowing,
and your vats will brim over with new wine.

Proverbs 3:9–10

Certainly the concept is relative. In the days of Solomon as now, a farmer with a thousand acres or a farmer with ten both have some measure of "firstfruits." The text likely refers to Old Testament law that required the Israelites to give the priests the first parts of oil, wine, and grain produced each year (Lev. 23:10; Num. 18:12–13).

Apparently part of wisdom means teaching our children generosity, a behavioral trait we must also model. We dare not cheat God by not being generous with him even though our salaries may be low, and we dare not cheat our children by not teaching them this significant emphasis in God's Word.

A mom tells this humorous story in *Reader's Digest:*

I was playing tooth fairy when my daughter, Shelby, suddenly woke up. Seeing the money in my hand, she cried out, "I caught you!"

I froze and tried to think of an explanation for why I—instead of the tooth fairy—was putting the money under her pillow. But her next words let me off the hook.

"You put that money back!" she said indignantly. "The tooth fairy left that for me!"[3]

Don't Forget the Value of Discipline

How interesting that a text that begins on the subject of wisdom should end with the subject of discipline:

My son, do not despise the LORD's discipline
and do not resent his rebuke,
because the LORD disciplines those he loves,
as a father the son he delights in.

Proverbs 3:11–12

Since we treated discipline in a previous chapter, we'll touch on it only lightly here. How important to remember that life does not consist only of healthy joints and full wine vats. The Father's children, both we and our children, must neither despise nor resent heavenly discipline. These verses (quoted in Heb. 12:5–6) emphasize that suffering affirms our role in the family. This is just another way God provides wisdom and keeps us on that straight path of verse 6.

Let's be careful; not all of life's struggles can be chalked up to God's discipline. Indeed, it would be quite inappropriate to identify the suffering of another as evidence of God's discipline in that life. Mature Christians understand that so much of what happens in their lives must be attributed strictly to the sovereignty of God, and they assume God knows what he is doing and why he is doing it.

Jeff's Story

Perhaps the greatest need for fatherly wisdom comes when a child prepares to launch from the nest. My senior year of high school brought the usual decisions about college. But since my father was the president of the only Christian college in the city, my choice seemed like a foregone conclusion.

But in wisdom, my dad talked with me about all my options. He ordered catalogs from other colleges. He didn't push or prod. He listened to me and counseled me, but he didn't assume or presume. He waited patiently for his maturing son to put some of his own wisdom into practice.

In the end, I did attend that Bible college in Miami, Florida. What I thought would be just a two-year associate degree ended up as a bachelor's degree in church ministries when God called me into full-time ministry. Sometimes fatherly wisdom demands that we allow our children to seek God's wisdom for themselves.

Kenn's Story

With no paternal mentor, I learned to stumble into wisdom one step at a time, often through difficult experience. In his grace, God taught me early the need for my complete dependence on him and the importance of generosity, particularly financial giving to churches and Christian organizations. My own undisciplined life may have caused an overreaction on the subject of wisdom, which I value highly and am often too harsh on others who seem, by my standards, to neglect it. Thank God that in the absence of an earthly father, the heavenly Father taught me that he will bring into my life only the things that are for my good. I have learned that he is not just the King of all the earth but a loving Father who wants his children on the safe path of secure fellowship with him.

Making It Work

Often when someone sneezes, coughs, or sniffs, he or she will say something like, "Oh, don't worry. I don't have a cold; it's just allergies." Well, "just allergies" cost Americans approximately four billion dollars a year. Children miss a collective two million school days every year and visit the doctor an average of 8.4 times a year because of allergies. The point? Don't minimize things that may seem obvious. To say that fathers need wisdom may evoke a mere nod of agreement and the thought: *Every idiot knows that.* But the amount of space that Scripture gives to this subject should drive us to our Bibles and our knees to seek exactly the quality Solomon describes in the Proverbs 3 passage.

So how can we practically bless our children with the gift of wisdom?

- Make note of lessons you have learned "the hard way" and communicate those stories to your children.
- When appropriate, allow your children to see you struggle through a decision-making process. Let them hear you pray for wisdom.
- Honor God with your finances. Your children will see their most visible example of spiritual wisdom in the way you handle your wallet.
- As they earn the right, allow your children to exercise their acquired wisdom.

Questions for Discussion

1. What are some of the ways you have used to pass on your values to your children? Describe some of those teachable moments.
2. What is the difference between worldly wisdom for fathering and godly wisdom for fathering? Give a few examples.
3. Why is it so important to seek wisdom in the way we handle our money and possessions?
4. Talk about one area of your fathering life in which you may need to ask God for more wisdom.

Father/Child Dialogue

1. Dad, explain the word *wisdom* to your children. Read from the Book of Proverbs using a children's Bible, something like *The Bible for Children*, which offers a simplified version of *The Living Bible* text. If they're older, try Eugene Peterson's *The Message*.
2. Kids, ask Dad if you can be wise even though you are young. How can eight-, twelve-, and fifteen-year-olds make wise decisions? How does God's wisdom come into play when you are at school?

thirteen

Imitating Infinite Intimacy

Attribute: Intimacy
Texts: John 14 and 17
Characters: Jairus and Daughter

I think that love is the only spiritual power that can overcome the self-centeredness that is inherent in being alive. Love is the thing that makes life possible or, indeed, tolerable.

Arnold Toynbee

When Jeff was born, Betty and Kenn expected a daughter. Before the days of sonograms, surprise still ruled the delivery room. Names had been chosen in both genders, just in case, but Kenn wanted a girl first and he assumed his desire determined the outcome. God responded to that presumption by sending a darling baby boy—Jeff.

For two decades (1960s and 1970s), the Gangel family followed the traditional patterns of what most families did back in those ancient times before the earth's crust had hardened. Dads matched up with sons and mothers matched up with daughters. This didn't mean any less love or concern on the part of either parent for the child of the opposite gender, it just happened that way. Playing with dolls and going shopping are areas in which most fathers have neither training nor experience. This unfortunate distinction confuses us, however, since a father serves the whole family not just his boys. A biblical example of a father's concern for his daughter comes to us in the Gospel of Mark. In chapter 5 we read, "One of the synagogue rulers, named Jairus, came there. Seeing Jesus, he fell at his feet and pleaded earnestly with him, 'My little daughter is dying. Please come and put your hands on her so that she will be healed and live' " (Mark 5:22–23). We don't see the father and daughter together until the last scene, but his irrepressible love for her flows from every verse of this story.

This chapter focuses on intimacy, a word not normally connected with theological thinking. Yet throughout the New Testament, particularly in the teaching of Jesus, we see how God wants an intimate relationship with us as our Father. We're aware that the word *intimacy* does not often show up in masculine vocabulary, but we believe that intimacy should be part of every father/child relationship.

Intimacy with Dignity

As Mark tells the story, Jairus comes off as a respected professional and well-known citizen with a strong interest in religion, and he has enough faith in Jesus to run to him during a crisis in his family. His twelve-year-old daughter had apparently been sick for a long time. Death seemed imminent. Anyone who has seen his child sick enough to discuss the possibility of death understands the agony and fear Jairus carried with him to Capernaum that day. Stu Weber puts it this way.

> We do not know the attitude of this synagogue ruler before his daughter's illness and death, but desperation can soften even the strongest critics. This man, like all the rest of the seekers in Matthew 8–9, was at the end of his resources. He had no place to turn except to the king. The official showed reverence for Jesus. Recognizing him as a prophet from God, the official knelt before him.[1]

Dignity almost turned to despair when Jesus stopped while on the way to Jairus's home to treat a woman "who had been subject to bleeding for twelve years" (Mark 5:25). We won't get into this story-within-a-story, but let's have a look at Jairus standing somewhere close to Jesus as this discussion of the woman's problem dragged on. Imagine his frustration. After all, he was a titled man and a leading citizen of that town. His life lay in shambles because of his daughter's illness, and he had thrown away his decorum to come and beg this amazing prophet to help. Now he saw only delay.

Something about the masculine ego constantly gravitates toward independence. Independence leads us to run to God only in crisis. Independence makes us irritable at standing in lines when we're in a hurry. Independence causes us to balk at sharing authority and decision making in the family. Yet the Bible constantly reminds us that God's work in our lives requires *dependence.* Rather than acting like know-it-all hotshots, spiritual fathers who are following the Bible understand and even verbalize their own struggles and weaknesses. This very attitude is a huge step toward intimacy with God (reaching up) and with the family (reaching out).

Let's face it—sometimes dads have no human answers for bewildering questions and no quick fixes for family problems. That's when we go to the heavenly Father and say, "Please help me." The ultimate blow for Jairus comes in verse 35: "While Jesus was still speaking, some men came from the house of Jairus, the synagogue ruler. 'Your daughter is dead,' they said. 'Why bother the teacher anymore?' " Perhaps just as Jairus began to lose his dignity, his hope, and perhaps even his faith, Jesus said, "Don't be afraid; just believe."

Intimacy with Deity

During the years our family lived in Miami, Florida, our attorney was a fine gentleman by the name of Hugh Carrier. The Carrier family lived in Coral Gables, and when Hugh's son Chris was ten years old, he was abducted. For weeks friends of the family and Christians all over the Miami area prayed for Chris Carrier, but no one knew where he was or what had happened to him. Sometime later we learned that the kidnapper, angry with the Carrier family for some reason, burned Chris with cigarettes, stabbed him numerous times with an ice pick, then shot him in the head and left him to die in the Everglades. Remarkably Chris survived, though he lost the sight in one eye. No one was ever arrested.

About five years ago, an old man confessed to the crime—David McAllister, a seventy-seven-year-old ex-convict, frail and blind, then living in a North Miami Beach nursing home. Meanwhile, Chris Carrier had grown up, trained for the ministry, and was now a youth pastor at Granada Presbyterian Church in his home city of Coral Gables. When he learned about McAllister, Chris began visiting him often, reading from the Bible, and praying for him. His personal care and ministry opened the door for McAllister to make a profession of faith.

There was no arrest, of course. After twenty-two years the statute of limitations had long passed. But that didn't bother Chris, since his motive had nothing to do with revenge or even justice but rather forgiveness. He puts it this way: "Though many people can't understand how I could forgive David McAllister, from my point of view I couldn't NOT forgive him. If I'd chosen to hate him all these years, or spent my life looking for revenge, then I wouldn't be the man I am today, the man my wife and children love, the man God has helped me to be."

Chris Carrier could act like that because he knows God intimately. He understands the meaning of John 16:27: "The Father himself loves you because you have loved me and have believed that I came from God."

According to John's record, Jesus spoke often about the Father but never more than in chapter 14 where the word *Father* appears twenty-two times, thirteen of them in the first fourteen verses. Yes, the chapter talks also about heaven, but let us not think of Jesus' preparation of heaven as a return to his carpentry skills, pounding boards in a housing project for believers. Forget the mansions; this passage talks about the personal touch of God on the lives of people. Jesus says, "I am the way and the truth and the life. No one comes to the Father except through me. If you really knew me, you would know my Father as well" (John 14:6–7). Philip raises doubt about the whole promise of heaven and the Lord's return and says, "Lord, show us the Father and that will be enough for us" (14:8).

Like the disciples, we do not know Jesus well enough, and therefore we struggle to understand the Father. Repeatedly Jesus emphasized the link between the heavenly Father and the Son, but right up to the end, the disciples did not get it. If we persist in seeing only God's power, eternality, and control over his world, we can never capture intimacy with deity.

What is God like? A certain pastor once gave a sermon on this topic. He talked on and on about God being like flowers, sunsets, the cry of a newborn baby, the beauty of a clear blue sky. Certainly, all those reflect God's natural revelation and therefore depict him, but that sermon never got to the bottom line: God is like Jesus Christ. That thought spins us into our next section.

Intimacy with Depth

Chuck Swindoll talks about men being tough and tender.

> That's the way my friend Joyce Landorf describes what every woman wants in a man. Her plea is for a balanced blend, an essential mixture of strong stability *plus* consideration, tact, understanding, and compassion. A better word is *gentleness*. But for some peculiar reason it is alien to the masculine temperament.[2]

The great father/child model of intimacy is found in the bond between God the Father and God the Son. We saw it in John 14; here it is again in chapter 17:

> My prayer is not for them alone. I pray also for those who will believe in me through their message, that all of them may be one, Father, just as you are in me and I am in you. May they also be in us so that the world may believe that you have sent me. I have given them the glory that you gave me, that they may be one as we are one: I in them and you in me. May they be brought to complete unity to let the world know that you sent me and have loved them even as you have loved me.
>
> John 17:20–23

The union of the family is not patterned after some earthly organization or some well-meaning intentions of humanity.

God joins our collective spirits through the Holy Spirit because Jesus' blood is "thicker than water" and thicker than human bonds. What the Lord prays about believers certainly applies to families as well—"that they may be one as we are one" (v. 22). Our intimacy with God is like a set of matched mixing bowls—we are the smaller one that fits into Christ who fits into the Father.

Dennis Rainey advises pastors and church leaders:

> Stress three key steps to marital oneness: purity and repentance, sanctity of the marriage covenant, and honoring God-ordained roles of husband and wife. These are essential not only to a good marriage but also to developing healthy, God-fearing children. Children experience great emotional insecurity when they see or experience disunity or coldness in their parents' marriages.[3]

One other scene of intimacy appears when Jesus casts himself as the Good Shepherd in John 10. He says, "I am the good shepherd; I know my sheep and my sheep know me—just as the Father knows me and I know the Father—and I lay down my life for the sheep" (vv. 14–15). The intimate relationship between Jesus and the Father provides the foundation for Christ's intimate relationship with us. Jesus knows everything about his sheep and loved them enough to die for them. How well do you know the little sheep God has entrusted to your fold?

We ended chapter 11 with a song; let's try it again. While Kenn might reach back for Bing Crosby and Jeff grab Chicago, we can come together at Barry Manilow, at least this particular song.

> We walked to the sea, just my father and me;
> And the dogs played around on the sand.
> Winter cold cut the air, hangin' still everywhere,
> Dressed in gray . . . did he say, "Hold my hand"?
> I said, "Love's easier when it's far away";
> We sat and watched a distant light.
>
> We're two ships that pass in the night,
> We both smile and we say it's all right;
> We're still here—it's just that we're out of sight
> Like those ships that pass in the night.

There's a boat on the line where the sea meets the sky,
There's another that rides far behind;
And it seems you and I are like strangers
A wide ways apart as we drift on through time.
He said, "It's harder now, we're far away
We only read you when you write";

We're two ships that pass in the night . . .[4]

———∞———

Jeff's Story

Intimacy takes on many forms in our family. Sometimes we will observe a family day when we schedule an outing or activity that involves only our family. We may hike, shop, drive, picnic, or all of the above. The bottom line—we intentionally spend time together as a family. As a result, we sing the same songs, we play the same games, we know the same inside jokes, and most important, we worship the same God. Just this morning we got up at 5:00 A.M. to sit on our driveway together and watch a meteor shower. We made a memory and tightened the bonds of family intimacy.

For me, bedtime provides the best intimacy-building moments. We always pray together as a family. Then it's Dad's time! I can't tell you everything we do (but then that's the nature of intimacy, right?). I can tell you that a combination of talking and wrestling each night has helped to keep me intimately attached to the hearts of my kids, so much so that this bedtime tradition endures even though my children are thirteen and fifteen. Intimacy won't just happen; you must make time and space for it in your life.

Kenn's Story

As an older man, I feel less than completely comfortable with the openness and frequency with which younger adults discuss matters of intimacy. Contemporary television sitcoms seem to distort and corrupt the privacy of family life.

Yet I have learned intimacy during fifteen years of empty nesting. What I had considered somewhat of a one-sided dependence of my family on me, I now see as a complete interdependence among all of us. What I once thought an almost burdensome responsibility of manhood, I now find a refreshing opportunity to share with vulnerability.

Nowhere is this more obvious than with my wife, Betty. Our relationship, always strong, has blossomed in recent years to a new recognition of how completely we need each other. That has become genuine intimacy—a gift of God to us and any couple who will accept it.

Making It Work

Meanwhile, back at Jairus and his daughter, we find a happy ending to the story. Mark tells us that Jesus "took her by the hand and said to her, *'Talitha koum!'* (which means, 'Little girl, I say to you, get up!'). Immediately the girl stood up and walked around. . . . At this they were completely astonished" (Mark 5:41–42). Seven people watched the miracle in the room that day including Peter, James, and John. Whatever Jairus had hoped for, it certainly did not include a resurrection, because he was as surprised as everyone else in the room. We could draw many practical lessons from the John passages we looked at in this chapter, but let's restrict ourselves just to the lessons we learn from Jairus.

- Don't allow your status outside the home to dilute your fathering, particularly in terms of your intimacy with your children.
- Remember that intimacy creates one of the sustaining pillars of the family in times of crisis.
- However difficult to maintain, intimacy is always worth the cost. The close relationship you develop with your daughter will impact her view of that future man in her life.
- Accept and live by the code that family life without Jesus is futile for Christian dads.

After buying movie tickets for his girlfriend and himself, a young man went over to the popcorn stand while his girlfriend went in to find seats. By the time he got through the line, the theater was dark and the previews had begun. Fumbling down the aisle, he finally found a seat, put down the popcorn, and gave his girlfriend a big kiss. Precisely at that moment he heard a familiar voice a couple of rows behind him say, "John, I'm back here."

Like that gal at the theater, many wives and children want to scream at Dad and say, "I'm back here!" Wherever our family is, we need to find them. And when we do, we need to make sure we never lose them again.

Questions for Discussion

1. Write a definition of *intimacy* (and don't say "the state of being intimate").
2. What opportunities do you foresee in the next month that will allow you to show intimacy to your wife and children?
3. If you were Jairus holding your daughter after Jesus brought her back from the dead, what would you say to her?

Father/Child Dialogue

1. Dad, tell your kids in simple terms how much you love them and how much they mean to you. By the way, according to Webster being *intimate* is "belonging to or characterizing one's deepest nature; marked by a very close association, contact or familiarity, marked by a warm friendship developing through long association."
2. Kids, tell Dad how much you love him and ask him about how and when he knew he was in love with Mom.

fourteen

A Worthy Investment

Attribute: Trustworthiness
Text: 2 Samuel 7:28–29
Characters: The Servants

Trust is a treasured item in a relationship. Once it is tarnished, it is hard to restore to its original glow.

William Ward

In Hanover, Germany, a bishop of the evangelical Lutheran church has designed what he calls a "separation ceremony" in which divorcing couples can publicly and formally renounce their vows as their children look on. The theory behind the service argues that if people involve God in the union, why shouldn't he also be involved in the split? The bishop claims that it is important to tell God when we fail. The public ceremony therefore provides both the elements of confession and absolution.

Maybe so. But there is a better solution—keep your promises from the beginning. Betty and Kenn have often been asked whether they've ever thought about divorce in their forty-seven years of marriage. Their stock answer is, "No, never; murder maybe, but never divorce."

In 2 Samuel 7:28 King David proclaims the trustworthiness of God: "O, Sovereign LORD, you are God! Your words are trustworthy, and you have promised these good things to your servant." Then he spread that blanket of blessing over his entire family in the very next verse: "Now be pleased to bless the house of your servant, that it may continue forever in your sight; for you, O Sovereign Lord, have spoken, and with your blessing the house of your servant will be blessed forever" (v. 29).

As we did with the other qualities, first we look at trustworthiness as an attribute of God. God's trustworthiness looks a bit different from ours, since he never changes. James Montgomery Boice writes, "The fact that God is eternal has two major consequences for us. The first is that *he can be trusted* to remain as he reveals himself to be. The word usually used to describe this quality is immutability, which means unchangeableness (James 1:17)."[1]

The Bible consistently calls for our response of trust to this primary characteristic of God. Jesus noted the failure of the son who promised to obey but could not be trusted to follow through (Matt. 21:28–31). For this chapter we will use Jesus' story of the investing servants in Luke 19. The spiritual lesson, as we shall see, emphasizes God's desire to trust his servants and his expectation of trustworthiness in his servants. Our practical application reminds us how a father must be trustworthy, a man of his word, so that he encourages trustworthiness in his children.

Jesus told the parable of the minas "because he was near Jerusalem and the people thought that the kingdom of God was going to appear at once" (v. 11). People did not grasp the time span between the first and second comings of the Lord, and the parable explains that. We need not focus primarily on the prophetic elements of the parable but rather learn what this story says to dads about their lives and relationship to Jesus the King.

Exhortation to Trustworthiness

We find historical background for this parable in the visit of Archelaus, son of Herod the Great, who went to Rome to obtain permission to reign as a client king over a territory actually subject to Rome (4 b.c.). The petition was opposed by a delegation of his subjects. Jesus' audience would have some familiarity with the kind of political intrigue the parable describes.

As in all parables about people, we try to identify the characters. First, we meet the *sovereign* who actually does not become a king until later in the story. At the beginning of the story, he is called "a man of noble birth." Next, we have the *servants*. This group should help us see ourselves; we are the servants of the King to whom he has given gifts and "talents" for use in his service.

Since one mina equaled one hundred drachmas, with each drachma worth about a day's wage, the total amount was worth between two and three years' average wages. The tenth (he gave each servant one mina) would be worth about three months' wages. Unlike the parable of the talents in Matthew 25, here all ten servants receive equal amounts, with the command, "Put this money to work."

But we find a third group of people here called *subjects*. In context, this group seems to represent the religious leaders of Israel and perhaps even the nation in general. Jesus was the King of the Jews; that title may have provoked scandalous scoffing at the cross, but it fit the eternal plan of the heavenly Father. Like the nation of Israel when the Lord came at his first advent, the subjects of the parable hated the king and sent their own representatives off to a foreign nation to say, "We don't want this man to be our king."

In this story Jesus is the sovereign and we are the servants. The subjects represent anyone who has rejected the gospel from the first century to the twenty-first. Fathers who are Christians, then, are also servants. This raises an interesting parallel with the headship theme we talked about earlier—interesting but not contradicting. The New Testament proclaims that genuine leaders act like servants, and in this parable we see that servants must be trustworthy. Proverbs 20:6 asks a fascinating question: "Many a man proclaims his own loyalty, but who can find a trustworthy man?"

Examination of Trustworthiness

When the nobleman was crowned king and returned home, he called in the servants to demand an account of the trust he had given them. He learned that one servant had earned 1,000 percent and a second 500 percent. But a third had only the original mina to return along with the rationale that taking a risk was imprudent because of the king's harsh reputation. Each servant receives a reward commensurate with his achievement—ten cities to the first and five cities to the second. We don't need to know about the other seven servants, for we already see the point of the parable. The amount is not the issue; what is being tested is obedience and the willingness to take risks in the aggressive and ambitious service of the master. We cannot summarize this parable by saying, "Nothing ventured; nothing gained." Rather the conclusion must be, "Nothing ventured; all lost." But we are getting ahead of the story.

The focus of the parable centers on the third servant who said, "Sir, here is your mina; I have kept it laid away in a piece of cloth" (v. 20). It's interesting that Jesus dispensed with the two faithful servants quite quickly, and we find ourselves focusing attention on the failing servant. How interesting here to find the focus on failure not on levels of success! It reminds us again that we need to keep our eyes off the numbers game and focus on our *dependability* and *trustworthiness*. God is watching us fathers. He's checking to see whether we read the handbook, interpret it correctly, and apply it consistently.

The 2000 census report counted 281,421,906 Americans, a 13-percent increase over the last decade. But the population curve didn't lean toward California and Florida, as we have come to expect; people are heading to Idaho, Utah, Colorado, Arizona, and Nevada, which grew 66.3 percent in the last ten years! Of course, American population growth is nothing compared to Asian and African statistics. But we do well to remember that God does not lose track of people when they move. Someday you and I will account for the way we handled the ministry of fathering, and trustworthiness will be close to the top of the list.

Expectation of Trustworthiness

Here's the warning in Jesus' own words.

His master replied, "I will judge you by your own words, you wicked servant! You knew, did you, that I am a hard man, taking

out what I did not put in, and reaping what I did not sow? Why
then didn't you put my money on deposit, so that when I came
back, I could have collected it with interest?"
   Then he said to those standing by, "Take his mina away from
him and give it to the one who has ten minas."
   "Sir," they said, "he already has ten!"
   He replied, "I tell you that to everyone who has, more will be
given, but as for the one who has nothing, even what he has will
be taken away."

Luke 19:22–26

One would think if the third servant really feared the master's autocratic leadership, he would at least have banked the
mina and had it available with whatever minor interest one could
get at the time. At least then he would have been able to return
more than he had received.
   In the original setting, or even in the kingdom parables of
Matthew 13, whether a person has little or much simply depends
on his use of opportunities to increase what God has given him.
Notice the king did not admit the accuracy of the servant's explanation; he did not agree that he was a hard man. But he does
say that if that's what the servant believed, then he should have
behaved differently.
   That's the key. Very few Christian fathers fail because they
don't believe in fathering or because they don't believe it ought
to have high priority in their lives. They fail because they *don't
translate belief into behavior.* Talking about it, reading about it,
even praying about it all have merit, but in the end, relationship
with family members is what really counts. Those relationships
are our minas, and we must invest our time in them on a daily
basis.
   Before we leave the parable, let's not miss the fact that Luke
records it just before the triumphal entry. A warning about how
to respond to the king appears just before the King offers himself to the nation. The application seems obvious and twofold.
To subjects, the parable says never reject the King whom God
has appointed. For servants, the parable contains a reminder to
faithfully account for all the Master has placed in our hands and
be ready to surrender it back to him with maximal interest at
his return.

What's the secret to trustworthiness in marriage and family life? As we have said numerous times in these chapters, placing family at the highest priority (even before your ministry at church) will launch you one big step forward. Another step is to treat marriage and fatherhood as the covenants they really are. Dennis Rainey reminds us:

> Although the concept of covenant was long implied in the Christian marriage ceremony, it wasn't until the fourteenth century in Northern France and England that the typical wedding ceremony included marriage vows (more accurately called "vow" because it was recited only by the husband). This example of such an early vow clearly reveals covenant concepts: "I take you as my wife, and I espouse you; and I commit to you the fidelity of my body, insofar as I bear for you fidelity and loyalty of my body and my possessions; and I will keep you in health and sickness and in any condition which it pleases our Lord that you should have, nor for the worse or for better will I change towards you until the end."[2]

Those archaic words fascinate us for two reasons. First, the single vow that places the burden of trustworthiness on the husband, though dramatically different from anything we would do today, certainly emphasizes the husband's leadership role in the home. We simply cannot abdicate God-ordained responsibilities.

But also the words "nor for the worse or for better will I change towards you" take us right back to the immutability of God on which the whole concept of trustworthiness rests. We are not only dependable men because it helps the family work better, our integrity reflects the person and work of God in Christ in our lives.

And children have a desperate desire to trust their parents. Here is one grandmother's illustration of that:

> My granddaughter Tyler's dangling front tooth was finally jarred loose by a jelly sandwich.
>
> The next morning at school, she eagerly showed off the money that was left under her pillow. "Tyler," a more worldly classmate informed her, "your mother is the tooth fairy!"
>
> "Is it true that you're the tooth fairy?" Tyler asked, confronting her mother that afternoon.

My daughter, Tracy, hugged her and replied, "Well, yes, honey, I am."

Tyler was stunned. "How could you do that?" she demanded. "How could you go out every night as the tooth fairy and leave me here all alone?"[3]

We know God is trustworthy because he is true. Jeremiah contrasts the heavenly Father's nature with that of the many false gods of the pagans all around him by calling him "the true God" (10:10). Jesus says "the only true God" in his Garden prayer (John 17:3). Laney tells us:

> The fact that God is true suggests that those who identify themselves with him by faith need to be real, genuine, and truthful in their relationships with others. Avoiding manipulation and "double-speak," they must "speak truth" to each other (Eph. 4:25, NASB). Also we need to represent God truly in our actions and in our behavior.[4]

Jeff's Story

Although most kids exhibit a natural childlike trust in their parents from earliest years, they also fall prey to some natural childhood doubts. Our daughter, Lyndsey, demonstrated unfounded fears of abandonment during her preschool years. Those doubts usually surfaced at bedtime. Invariably, as Beth and I would turn off her light and partially close the door, Lyndsey's cute little voice would peep, "Are you staying inside all the time?"

We had never left her "home alone," yet her tender emotions needed the assurance that we would stay in the family room while she went to sleep. Solid trust must be earned. Lyndsey doesn't ask that question anymore. Years of *staying there* has produced the trust that her dad will always be available to her.

Dads prove themselves trustworthy through *consistency*. We must look for every opportunity to demonstrate dependability, and then do it every time. By the way, even if that trust has been broken or compromised in some way in the past, you can rebuild your trustworthiness through consistency now.

Kenn's Story

Quite frankly, I was so in love with my wife before and after the time of our wedding that I never thought about the details. We recited the old-fashioned vows and assumed, I guess, that they would carry us to the end of our lives. I'm afraid too often independence took my attention off family priorities. Workaholic tendencies have attempted to strangle me for forty-five years, and I fear that even in retirement I am unable to shake off their tentacles.

The turning point came about ten years ago when a variety of health problems pushed me into the interdependent relationship with my wife I described in the last chapter. Funny how God uses different things to shape our spiritual character. My admission of need, to myself, to God, and to my wife, brought about a whole new focus of understanding that trustworthiness means more than just moral purity and a willingness to keep the bank account balanced.

Making It Work

Let's have another look at Matthew 21, a text we mentioned at the beginning of the chapter. Verses 28–31 contain the brief parable about two sons who said one thing and did another.

> "What do you think? There was a man who had two sons. He went to the first and said, 'Son, go and work today in the vineyard.'
> 'I will not,' he answered, but later he changed his mind and went.
> "Then the father went to the other son and said the same thing. He answered, 'I will, sir,' but he did not go.
> "Which of the two did what his father wanted?"
> "The first," they answered.
> Jesus said to them, "I tell you the truth, the tax collectors and the prostitutes are entering the kingdom of God ahead of you."

The Lord ends the story with a rhetorical question and his opponent answers correctly. But neither son behaved with trustworthiness. What we need in this parable is a son who agrees to work in the vineyard and then goes out and works in the vineyard. Weber puts this little story in context.

Jesus had struck the first of three blows against the credibility of the leaders of Israel—against their qualification to serve as the shepherds of God's people. In spite of the religious show they put on and their claims to be obedient to God, they had rejected the mission God had given them. . . . They were guilty of neglect and abuse of God's flock.[5]

Neglect and abuse happen when dads are not trustworthy. How can we solve the problem?

- Dig through the archives drawer until you find your marriage covenant and review it. Better yet, have a look at the video of your marriage ceremony if you have one.
- Understand that trustworthiness is impossible over the long haul without the constant assistance of the Holy Spirit in our lives. God brings us to faith, God sustains our faith, and God alone can make us trustworthy men.
- Form an accountability group with two or three other guys. This could be with a grown son or sons, fellow believers at church, or Christian men you know in another context. Allow someone to hold your nose to the grindstone on the issue of family trustworthiness.

David Seamans, author and professor at Asbury Seminary, tells a story about when the seminary shared cafeteria facilities with Asbury College in Wilmore, Kentucky. On one occasion, students moving through the cafeteria line found near the beginning a large basket of bright red apples. The cafeteria staff had placed a sign above the basket, quite appropriate for a Christian college campus, "Take only one, please—God is watching."

As students made their way through the line, selecting meat loaf or taco salad, peaches, and chocolate mousse, they found at the other end a large box of broken cookies that the staff had put out. Attached to the box was a piece of notebook paper containing a note obviously scrawled by a student. It read, "Take as many as you want. God is watching the apples."

Yes, God is watching the apples, but God is watching the cookies too. God is watching our children, but God is watching us as well.

Questions for Discussion

1. Think about the men you consider to be genuinely trustworthy in their homes, jobs, and churches. What qualities do they have in common?
2. Now do exactly the same thing with the men you consider less than trustworthy or even devious. What similarities do you see in them?
3. Discuss what you think would happen if you asked your wife and your children to tell you (in fairly specific terms) how you could be a better father. Then actually ask them!

Father/Child Dialogue

1. Dad, tell your kids why the family is your highest priority after your personal relationship with God, and then tell them what your hopes are for them when they become adults.
2. Kids, can your parents trust you at all times, even when they can't see you? Tell your dad why he can trust you.

fifteen

A Few Good Men

Attribute: Goodness
Text: Psalm 34:8
Characters: Joseph and Jesus

Most men are not as good as they pretend to be, nor as bad as
their enemies paint them.

Morris Abram

Military slogans have always offered interesting sound bites—
Join the Navy and See the World; Uncle Sam Needs You; Today's
Army Serves You. But for decades now the Marines have stuck
with a simple slogan emphasizing their focus on quality rather
than quantity—A Few Good Men. *Good* is an interesting choice
of adjective, isn't it? Why not say a few brave men? Or a few
courageous leaders? Apparently the Marines believe simple is
better and so they tell us they are looking for *good men*.

Most women too will tell you that good men are hard to find.
And when they use that expression, they seem to know (at least
among themselves) what they mean. Since men rarely know
what women are thinking, an analysis of goodness seems worth
some time and thought in this book. Discovering "what women
want" can be embarrassing and humiliating as well as exciting.

Knowing what God wants, on the other hand, should be a constant quest for every Christian man, especially those engaged in the ministry of fathering.

Some attributes of God (omnipotence, omnipresence, omniscience) belong to him alone. Many others, however, can be reflected in earthly fathers, and *goodness* is in that second category. Psalm 34:8 tells us, "Taste and see that the LORD is good; blessed is the man who takes refuge in him." In Psalm 119:68 we read, "You are good, and what you do is good." What a desirable attribute! What man wouldn't want his wife and children to apply those words to him?

In this chapter we want to pick up that theme and apply it to human fathers. If even the Marines are looking for good men, we can only assume that God wants to find in us a biblical reflection of this divine attribute. Our biblical example for this chapter focuses on the man God chose to be the earthly father of Jesus—Joseph the carpenter from Nazareth.

Good Men Are Righteous

Joseph represents one of the few examples of positive fathering we see in either Testament. His name means "may God add," a name commonly used by the Jews from the earliest days of the patriarchs and not uncommon in the twenty-first century. In his role as the legal father of Jesus, Joseph lived out a principle that we see explained and expanded with enthusiasm in later pages of the New Testament—*leadership begins at home.* As a single, blue-collar worker in Nazareth, Joseph seemed unimportant and doubtless attracted little attention. But in his role as a father who exhibited goodness, he has provided an example for more than two thousand years. The Greek word for *good* does not appear in this description of Joseph in Matthew 1, but the text certainly qualifies Joseph as our model, God's selection of an earthly father for his Son.

When Joseph learned of Mary's pregnancy and made the decision to cancel the engagement privately, Matthew says he did it because he "was a righteous man" (Matt. 1:19). The text indicates that Joseph knew nothing about Mary's encounter with the angel who revealed the miraculous conception to her. Nor, for some reason, had Mary mentioned it to Joseph. Theirs was a different culture; she simply rested in God's ability to communicate with Joseph as he had with her.

We can only imagine the heartbreak when this good man discovered his fiancée was already pregnant. His response is the most distinctive mark of his character shown us in all the pages of Scripture. As *a righteous man* he knew the law and the requirements for this kind of thing, but he did not use them as a weapon to punish Mary. Surely he felt indignation, frustration, and perhaps even anger because of the way he assumed Mary had wronged him. But he reacted in kindness, and in doing so he reflected two of the qualities perfectly embodied in his son. As John puts it, "The Word became flesh and made his dwelling among us. We have seen his glory, the glory of the One and Only, who came from the Father, full of grace and truth" (John 1:14).

How do we acquire righteousness that makes us good men? In both Old and New Testaments, biblical righteousness simply means thinking and acting in conformity with God's standard. The more we behave like God, the more righteous we are and therefore the more we reflect his goodness. Of course, whatever righteousness we have comes only from God's work in our lives through the Holy Spirit and represents only a shadow of his absolute righteousness. Paul put it clearly in his letter to the church at Philippi.

> But whatever was to my profit I now consider loss for the sake of Christ. What is more, I consider everything a loss compared to the surpassing greatness of knowing Christ Jesus my Lord, for whose sake I have lost all things. I consider them rubbish, that I may gain Christ and be found in him, not having a righteousness of my own that comes from the law, but that which is through faith in Christ—the righteousness that comes from God and is by faith.
>
> Philippians 3:7–9

The more we know God's Word, the better equipped we will be to choose righteousness as a way of life and function consistently as good men.

Good Men Are Obedient to God

In Matthew 1 we read the angel's message to Joseph, which contains the first of many Old Testament quotations in that book (Matt. 1:20–23). Sensitive to the leading of God in his life, Joseph became the privileged recipient of a visit by one of God's heavenly messengers. The angel tells Joseph the mystery of the virgin birth, the mystery of salvation, and the mystery of fulfilled prophecy. Every righteous Jew longed for that moment when God would break through human history to take charge of the world with the coming of Messiah. Now on a humble carpenter's cot in Nazareth, a young man learns that he will father this Yeshua, the Savior of the world.

It was quite a night! In one dream Joseph encountered the angelic messenger and learned that his virgin fiancée was with child, that the child was Messiah, and that all this fulfilled the exciting prophecy of Isaiah 7:14 with which, as a righteous Jew, he had been familiar all his life.

No man could easily push aside the staggering angelic message Joseph heard that night, though lesser men might have responded in different ways. For Joseph the obedience was instantaneous, second nature to the righteousness that marked his lifestyle: "When Joseph woke up, he did what the angel of the Lord had commanded him and took Mary home as his wife. But he had no union with her until she gave birth to a son. And he gave him the name Jesus" (Matt. 1:24–25). We assume the wedding took place immediately and that Joseph took on himself the stigma that Mary otherwise would have borne alone.

In the record of the Christmas story we learn that God came to live at Joseph's house. His name was Jesus, the Greek equivalent of the popular Hebrew name Joshua, meaning "Jehovah is salvation." But he was also called Immanuel, which means "God with us." What must Joseph have thought? How difficult would be his role in fathering like the Father? At Christmas we sing Charles Wesley's marvelous description of this first advent.

> Come, Thou long-expected Jesus,
> Born to set Thy people free;
> From our fears and sins release us;
> Let us find our rest in Thee.

Israel's Strength and Consolation,
Hope of all the earth Thou art;
Dear Desire of every nation,
Joy of every longing heart.

Good Men Protect Their Families

One of the tasks both of us take seriously is the role and duties of "chief security officer." It may sound old-fashioned and just a bit politically incorrect, but we cling to the notion that Dad is responsible for keeping the family out of trouble and protecting them in a dangerous environment. We go around and make sure the doors are all locked at night. We keep alert with eyes scanning the surroundings when the family walks through a high-crime area. We read maps and road signs so the family doesn't get lost on a vacation trip. (We also read maps so that we don't have to stop and ask anybody for directions.)

Joseph was that kind of protective father. After a brief record of the Magi visit in the opening verses of chapter 2, Matthew describes a second angelic message Joseph received—this time a warning.

> When they had gone, an angel of the Lord appeared to Joseph in a dream. "Get up," he said, "take the child and his mother and escape to Egypt. Stay there until I tell you, for Herod is going to search for the child to kill him."
>
> So he got up, took the child and his mother during the night and left for Egypt, where he stayed until the death of Herod. And so was fulfilled what the Lord had said through the prophet: "Out of Egypt I called my son."
>
> Matthew 2:13–15

In Matthew 2 Joseph is still the focal point of the record. His son's life had been threatened, so Joseph, assuming his role as protector of the family, took them to Egypt. This is an interesting choice in view of the historic enmity between Israel and Egypt. But we find the fulfillment of another prophecy here, which Joseph may have realized was becoming a pattern. This time the prophecy is found in Hosea 11:1, where we read: "When

Israel was a child, I loved him, and out of Egypt I called my son." Surely Old Testament believers took this verse as a historic reference to deliverance from Pharaoh, but now in Matthew we learn it serves as a prophecy that Joseph's son, the Messiah, would spend some time in Egypt as well.

Joseph didn't ask about the employment opportunities in Egypt. He moved quickly to protect his family. Like Joseph, modern fathers should reflect the heavenly Father's care of his children. Often, to do so, we find it necessary to challenge the corporate god of Western capitalism. Simply put, the family comes before the job—or the ministry.

Sometimes we walk a thin line between protection and overprotection. Obviously, as children grow, we deliberately begin to withdraw our authority, requiring them to make decisions based on their own knowledge of Scripture and their spiritual convictions. But this is a process not an event. If we don't protect our children during the early years, they may not be able to make right choices as teenagers and adults. And the protection does not deal only with physical danger or family safety. God expects us to protect our children from the world's infatuation with evil and its distortion of truth. Guarding against the intrusion of Satan through television, video games, and the Internet is surely as much a part of family protection as locking the doors or insisting that everybody fasten seat belts.

The role of protector fits in well with the biblical understanding of masculinity. The Bible tells us that God deliberately designed the sexes as male and female to establish the family (Genesis 1 and 2). In so doing, he ordained equality of essence and value but hardly uniformity of function. Scripture implies no inferiority by claiming that men and women are different in what God expects of them. Psychologists tell us that the failure of a male child to see a proper masculine image in his father will lead to all kinds of later distortions—from homosexuality to an inability to implement an appropriate fathering role in his own family.

Denying pagan egotism that applauds being born male instead of female, Christian fathers thank God for what we have become by his grace and what he may yet develop in us along the journey of faith. We recognize that masculinity brings enormous responsibility, not because of some superiority but because of the tasks God has given us. What more awesome responsibility could we have than recognizing that when God described his own goodness with his spiritual children, he referred to it as *fathering?*

Good Men Are Tender and Gentle

If we gave wives a list of qualities they want in their husbands, the terms *tender* and *gentle* would attract a lot of votes. Yet we do not commonly use these words to describe ourselves. We prefer words like *strong, courageous,* and *kind;* tender and gentle seem a bit too feminine. But the Bible applies these words to Jesus, and they also reflect Joseph's relationship with his wife and son.

In Matthew 2:19 Joseph receives yet a third angelic message and instantly obeys God's command to return to the land of Israel. We often think of Mary as the dominant parent in the relationship with Jesus, probably because she is there during his adult years. But a reading of the Gospels certainly indicates that the link between Joseph and Jesus was always marked by love and tenderness. Jesus could quite comfortably refer to the God of the universe as Father when he remembered the precious hours spent with Joseph in the carpenter's shop in Nazareth.

Let's remember too that one of the most important things a father can do for his children is to clearly show them how much he loves their mother. Showing tenderness and being sensitive to the woman we have covenanted to love and protect for life should hardly seem like strenuous or complicated work.

Teamwork is the key. Father and mother make up the most important team in the world (with the exception of husband and wife). When those combinations both operate at a reasonable level of competence, in accordance with biblical standards, they offer hope for society.

In the George Bernard Shaw stage play *St. Joan,* the author describes a coronation scene in Reims Cathedral in which Joan tells of hearing a voice calling her to deliver France. The weak King Charles interrupts, "Oh, your voices, your voices! Why don't the voices come to me? I am king, not you." Joan replies, "They do come to you; but you do not hear them. When the angel rings, you cross yourself and have done with it; but if you prayed from your heart, and listened to the trilling of the bells in the air after they stop ringing, you would hear the voices as well as I do."

Joseph heard voices in the night. Not through magic or wizardry but because he was a good man who listened to God. Unlike the Pharisees and many of the people of his day who wore religion as an external veneer, Joseph prayed from the heart and stayed in contact with God.

Not only does God call us to be good men, he offers to make that possible through his power. So let's acknowledge our *failures* but quickly surrender to our *faith*. Let's proclaim our *weakness* but ask God for adequate *wisdom*. Let's abandon the old image that a man should suppress his emotions and hurts so that he can get on with the job of solving everybody's problems. Biblical fathering requires us to do the very best we can with the resources God has given us. Ultimately we provide stability for the sheltering system our families desperately need in a shattered and shattering age. We are neither bionic nor moronic—just men—human beings trying to be what God wants us to be, often stumbling while trying to climb the mountain of goodness.

Jeff's Story

One Christmas I became Joseph. Well, only for a moment. Dramatizing the experience in a Christmas cantata, I sang "Joseph's Song," written by Michael Card. As I learned and sang the words, I gained a new appreciation for Joseph's situation.

> Father, show me where I fit into this plan of Yours.
> How can a man be father to the Son of God?
> Lord, for all my life I've been a simple carpenter.
> How can I raise a king?
> How can I raise a king?[1]

How overwhelmed Joseph must have felt at times!

Though God has not asked me to be father to his Son, he has given me two of his precious children to raise. I pray that goodness may mark my fathering.

Kenn's Story

I have always found myself drawn to Joseph in Matthew's Christmas narrative. I don't recall seeing any of the qualities of goodness in my own father, and I have been startled often by the father failure so evident in many Bible characters, even spiritual heroes like Abraham, Samuel, and David. Quite frankly, this one-two punch caused me in earlier years to wonder whether I could actually be a *good* man, a *good* father. God had to pull my sights away from other human fathers and focus them on him. He alone is the model. He alone is the pattern. And fathering like the Father is only possible because the Holy Spirit incarnates the life and love of the heavenly Father in us.

Making It Work

As we write this chapter, the Ford Motor Company is running a series of commercials targeted at tough guys who don't go to certain movies and never reflect a soft or tender side to their personality. Though the commercials do not actually say it, they also imply that these guys use abusive and vulgar language, care only about their own work and lives, and apply the word *good* only to food, beer, and sports.

Christian fathers should sense such distortion of masculinity in an instant. God wants us to be good men, and goodness can be both defined and described. How can we model goodness in our lives and families?

- Stay tuned to the Holy Spirit at all times. Acknowledge that if you are a believer, Jesus Christ lives in your heart through the Holy Spirit. The Spirit gives us wisdom to make key decisions for the family but also provides restraint on behaviors that would damage our ability to be good men.

• Ask God to make you a more sensitive and tender person. Be alert to the hurts and fears of your wife and children and let them know that they can depend on you to care for and protect them at all times.

• Model instant obedience for your family. We believe you should require that of your children, and they are much more likely to practice instant obedience if they see that you follow God's Word as soon as you know it through the reading of Scripture or through prayer.

And let's make sure that this is not some short-term pantomime we stage for the family's benefit. James once wrote of the heavenly Father, "Every good and perfect gift is from above, coming down from the Father of the heavenly lights, who does not change like shifting shadows" (James 1:17). Good men are *consistently* good, *consistently* righteous, *consistently* obedient, *consistently* protective, and *consistently* sensitive and caring with their families. It may take a miracle of God's grace to achieve this in your life, but God specializes in the miracle business.

Questions for Discussion

1. Rate yourself on a scale of righteousness from 1 to 10, with 10 representing the most righteous. Reflect on why you chose the number you did.
2. Name some reasons your wife and children would have for calling you a *good* man when they discuss you with other people.
3. How would you explain to your wife and children that you have decided to emphasize goodness more in your relationships with them?
4. At times you may play and wrestle with your children, but when and how do they see your tender, gentle side?

Father/Child Dialogue

1. Dad, talk with your children about what it must have been like to be the earthly father of Jesus and ask them what qualities they think Jesus may have wanted to see in Joseph.

2. Kids, tell your father why you think he is a good man and talk about some specific things he has said or done to show you that is true.

Conclusion

Oh, to be a father like the Father, a high calling, to be sure. Obviously this is a great challenge but most certainly a crying need. President Herbert Hoover put it in the form of a "want" ad:

> Immediate openings for an honorable job,
> With long hours and no time off—
> Must be willing to work all hours,
> Including the middle of the night,
> Weekends, holidays, and vacations.
> Requires survival traits, like strength and patience,
> Imagination, humor, and flexibility,
> Intelligence and understanding,
> And above all, a good heart.
> Must be a human being, kind and gentle,
> With basic goodness and fearlessness.
> Leadership qualities are necessary,
> And the ability to instruct and guide is a requirement.
> Receive on-the-job training, with no pay.
> There will be unpredictable surprises and rewards—
> Like joy, love, pain, fun, and many difficulties.
> Want a challenge? Be a dad!

We close with the words of a wonderful song recorded by Phillips, Craig, and Dean that sums up the message of this book. We pray this for ourselves and for you. It is the prayer of a father to his Father about his son.

> Lord, I want to be just like You
> 'Cause he wants to be just like me.

I want to be a holy example
For his innocent eyes to see.
I want to be a living Bible, Lord,
That my little boy can read.
I want to be just like You
'Cause he wants to be like me.
Right now from where he stands
I may seem mighty tall
But it's only 'cause I'm learning
From the best Father of them all.[1]

Notes

Chapter 1 *Make 'Em Laugh*

1. George Reckers, ed., *Family Building* (Ventura, Calif.: Regal, 1985), 84.
2. Erma Bombeck, *Family—the Ties That Bind . . . and Gag!* (New York: Fawcett, 1988), 2.
3. Charles Swindoll, *Laugh Again* (Nashville: Word, 1995), 14.

Chapter 2 *An Officer or a Gentleman?*

1. Charles Sell, *Unfinished Business: Helping Adult Children Resolve Their Past* (Portland, Ore.: Multnomah, 1989), 171.

Chapter 3 *Focus on the Father*

1. Charles Swindoll, *Man to Man* (Grand Rapids: Zondervan, 1996), 235.

Chapter 4 *The Ultimate Sacrifice*

1. Erma Bombeck, sermonillustrations.com/a-z/f/father.htm
2. Ross Campbell, *How to Really Love Your Child* (Wheaton: Victor, 1977), 29.

Chapter 5 *The Green-Eyed Monster?*

1. Charles Swindoll, *The Tale of the Tardy Oxcart* (Nashville: Word, 1998), 311–12.
2. Quoted in John Stott, *The Contemporary Christian* (Downers Grove, Ill.: InterVarsity Press, 1992), 95.
3. Crawford Lorritts Jr., "10 Ways to Be a Better Father," *AMF Newsletter* 6, no. 2 (October 1998).

Chapter 6 *Truth or Consequences*

1. Michael Phillips, *To Be a Father Like the Father* (Camp Hill, Pa.: Christian Publications, 1992), 297.
2. John MacArthur, *God* (Wheaton: Victor, 1993), 26–27.
3. Erwin Lutzer, *Ten Lies about God* (Nashville: Word, 2000), 27.

4. Douglas Groothuis, "How the Bombarding Images of T.V. Culture Undermine the Power of Words," *Modern Reformation* (January/February 2000), 37.

5. Chuck Colson, "Merchants of Cool," *Christianity Today* (11 June 2001), 112.

6. David Reiss et al., *The Relationship Code: Deciphering Genetic and Social Influences on Adolescent Development* (Cambridge: Harvard University Press, 2000), 64.

Chapter 7 *God's Friend*

1. Colin Powell, "In Father's Absence, Mentor Can Make the Difference," *St. Petersburg Times*, 20 June 1999, C3.

2. Josh McDowell, *The Disconnected Generation* (Nashville: Word, 2000), 114.

3. Carl Laney, *God* (Nashville: Word, 1999), 169.

4. Katy Kelly, "Child Docs to Parents: Stay Home and Save Your Kids," *U.S. News & World Report* 129, no. 17 (30 October 2000), 65.

5. Leonard Pitts, *Becoming Dad: Black Men and the Journey to Fatherhood* (New York: Longstreet, 1999).

6. Quoted in the *Dallas Morning News*, 7 March 1991, B1.

7. Laney, *God*, 175.

8. Quoted in the *Dallas Morning News*, 17 April 1992, A7.

9. Lloyd Cory, *Quotable Quotations* (Wheaton: Victor, 1985), 135.

Chapter 8 *The Child Whisperer*

1. Paul Randolph, *Journal of Biblical Counseling* (fall 1997), 15.

2. Alden Lynch, *Leadership* (spring 2000): 46.

Chapter 9 *Lessons from an Old Man*

1. Charles B. Flood, *Lee: The Last Years* (Boston: Houghton Mifflin, 1998), 236.

2. Theodore Seuss Geisel, from a commencement address at Lake Forest College.

3. A. W. Tozer, *The Knowledge of the Holy* (New York: Harper, 1861); Lewis Sperry Chafer *He That Is Spiritual* (Grand Rapids: Zondervan, 1918); Francis A. Schaeffer, *True Spirituality* (Wheaton, Ill.: Tyndale, 1971).

Chapter 10 *Winning the Game*

1. Steve Chapman, "Broken Pieces" (Dawn Treader Music, a Division of Jubilee Communications, 1982). International copyright secured. All rights reserved.

Chapter 11 *Find Us Faithful*

1. Laney, *God*, 91–92.

2. Charles Ryrie, *Basic Theology* (Wheaton: Victor, 1986), 39.

3. Michael Novak, *Harper's* (April 1976).

4. Jon Mohr, "Find Us Faithful" (Brentwood, Tenn.: ADM by Gaither Copyright Management and Birdwing Music, 1987).

Chapter 12 *A Gift from God*

1. A. W. Tozer, *The Knowledge of the Holy* (New York: Harper, 1961), 66.
2. Quoted in *Reader's Digest* (March 2001), 114.
3. Quoted in *Reader's Digest* (August 2001), 208.

Chapter 13 *Imitating Infinite Intimacy*

1. Stuart K. Weber, *Matthew*, Holman New Testament Commentary (Nashville: Broadman & Holman, 2000), 118.
2. Swindoll, *Man to Man*, 142.
3. Dennis Rainey, *Ministering to Twenty-First-Century Families* (Nashville: Word, 2001), 158.
4. Ian Hunter, "Ships" (SBK April Music Inc. and Ian Hunter Music, Inc., 1979). All rights controlled and administered by SBK April Music Inc. All rights reserved. International copyright secured.

Chapter 14 *A Worthy Investment*

1. James M. Boice, *The Sovereign God* (Downers Grove, Ill.: InterVarsity Press, 1978), 131.
2. Rainey, *Ministering to Twenty-First-Century Families*, 36.
3. Quoted in *Reader's Digest* (August 2001), 208.
4. Laney, *God*, 56.
5. Weber, *Matthew*, 346.

Chapter 15 *A Few Good Men*

1. Michael Card, "Joseph's Song" (Whole Armor Publishing/ASCAP, 1982).

Conclusion

1. Dan Dean and Joy Becker, "I Want to Be Just Like You" (Praise Song Press, ASCAP, Dawn Treader Music, 1994). All rights reserved.

Bibliography

Boice, James M. *The Sovereign God*. Downers Grove, Ill.: InterVarsity Press, 1978.

Campbell, Ross. *How to Really Love Your Child*. Wheaton: Victor, 1977.

Crabb, Larry. *Men and Women—Enjoying the Difference*. Grand Rapids: Zondervan, 1991.

Gangel, Kenn, and Betty Gangel. *Your Family*. Gresham, Ore.: Vision House, 1995.

Henslin, Earl R. *Man to Man*. Nashville: Thomas Nelson, 1993.

Laney, Carl. *God*. Nashville: Word, 1999.

Lutzer, Erwin. *Ten Lies about God*. Nashville: Word, 2000.

MacArthur, John. *God*. Wheaton: Victor, 1993.

McDowell, Josh. *The Disconnected Generation*. Nashville: Word, 2000.

Minirth, Frank, Brian Newman, and Paul Warren. *The Father Book: An Instruction Manual*. Nashville: Thomas Nelson, 1992.

Phillips, Michael E. *To Be a Father Like the Father*. Camp Hill, Pa.: Christian Publications, 1992.

Pitts, Leonard. *Becoming Dad: Black Men and the Journey to Fatherhood*. New York: Longstreet, 1999.

Rainey, Dennis. *Ministering to Twenty-First-Century Families*. Nashville: Word, 2001.

Reckers, George, ed. *Family Building*. Ventura, Calif.: Regal, 1985.

Reiss, David, et al. *The Relationship Code: Deciphering Genetic and Social Influences on Adolescent Development*. Cambridge: Harvard University Press, 2000.

Sell, Charles M. *Power Dads*. Ann Arbor, Mich.: Servant Publications, 1996.

———. *Unfinished Business: Helping Adult Children Resolve Their Past*. Portland, Ore.: Multnomah, 1989.

Simmons, Dave. *Dad the Family Mentor*. Wheaton: Victor, 1992.

Stott, John. *The Contemporary Christian*. Downers Grove, Ill.: InterVarsity Press, 1992.

Swindoll, Charles. *Laugh Again*. Nashville: Word, 1995.

———. *Man to Man*. Grand Rapids: Zondervan, 1996.

———. *The Strong Family*. Portland, Ore.: Multnomah, 1991.

Tozer, A. W. *The Knowledge of the Holy*. New York: Harper, 1961.

Weber, Stu. *Tender Warrior: God's Intention for a Man*. Portland, Ore.: Multnomah, 1993.

Williams, Charles. *Forever a Father (Always a Son)*. Wheaton: Victor, 1991.

Kenn and **Jeff Gangel** have many things in common besides writing books together. They both have master's degrees in Bible and theology; Kenn has a doctorate in education and Jeff a doctor of ministry degree. Kenn has been a professor at Trinity Evangelical Divinity School, vice president of Dallas Theological Seminary, and president of Miami Christian College. Jeff has served fifteen years as a pastor and is currently Vice President for Spiritual Formation at Toccoa Falls College in Georgia, where his father is Scholar-in-Residence.

Kenn and his wife, Betty, have two children, Jeff and Julie. Jeff and his wife, Beth, also have two children, Lyndsey and Bradley.